Switch

★

How To Think Differently And Unlock Your True Potential With NLP

NATALIE DEBRABANDERE

Copyright © 2015 Natalie Debrabandere

All rights reserved.

This book is sold subject to the condition that it shall not, by way of trade or otherwise, be lent, resold, hired out, reproduced or otherwise circulated without the author's prior consent in any form of binding or cover other than that in which it is published or without a similar condition, including this condition, being imposed on the subsequent purchaser.

Cover Design by BespokeBookCovers.com

www.switchonnlp.com

ISBN: 1514815427
ISBN-13: 9781514815427

DEDICATION

Dedicated to all the wonderful people out there who choose to be different; all of you who have the courage to follow your heart, challenge the rules, and live an authentic and meaningful life.

CONTENTS

- Acknowledgments — i
- Introduction — Pg 1
- Part One: Losing My Mind — Pg 7
- Part Two: NLP Nitty-Gritty — Pg 63
- Part Three: Top Tips For Living — Pg 111
- Conclusion — Pg 155
- Quotes — Pg 165
- Resources – books — Pg 167
- Resources – websites — Pg 168
- Definitions — Pg 169
- About the author — Pg 175

ACKNOWLEDGMENTS

A massive thank you goes to my friend Laura, for volunteering to be my first ever reader: thank you so much for your insightful feedback and ongoing support.

I would also like to thank the great team at Inspire 360, the UK's leading school of NLP training: Joanne, for giving me the opportunity to blog on your websites, and Ewan, for being a real model of excellence and doing such a great job of "showing me the door"! Colin and Craig, thank you both for your support on the Barcelona Trainers' Training, and helping me to find that bar!

Many thanks to Peter and Caroline at BespokeBookCovers.com, for designing a cover I am so proud of and making the whole process such an exciting and pleasurable experience.

Last but certainly not least, thank you to you, for reading my book; it means a lot to me, and I hope it will inspire you to reach for the stars!

INTRODUCTION

GET BUSY LIVING

In the film *The Shawshank Redemption*, Tim Robbins' character Andy Dufresne delivers the very famous line: "Get busy livin', or get busy dyin'."

We could do a few variations on the same theme, around and in between. Not getting busy doing either would be one, just to be awkward; or getting busy not dying… which for some people is clearly the main preoccupation of their entire lives.

I guess that's okay sometimes – can't deny that staying away from death or injury seems like a sensible approach, although never taking any risks could lead to a very boring existence; a sort of "non-life". You could be "not dead" and "not alive" both at the same time. You could be stuck essentially, suspended in mid-flow like a puzzled puppet.

What then? Well, you would have to realise that you are stuck first, which might be harder than you think since it tends to be the accepted norm in our society: eat, work, sleep, repeat, do not deviate under any circumstances. But if you were lucky enough to realise that you can live differently, you might want to do something about it. To get moving again, to get flowing again.

Now, what if you did not have the tools? What if you did not know which ones you needed? And what if you did have the tools, as we all do, but you did not know it, or even how to use them? More importantly, what if you believed this only because you did not believe it was possible in the first place?

One day at the office I used to work a bunch of people were talking about the EuroMillions rollover, and what they would do with the money if they won. Every single person said the first thing they would do was quit their current job, which was interesting to say the least!

One hard-core sales guy said he would open a bakery so he could make people feel good. A grumpy financial analyst said she would take care of all of her family and friends first, and then live a simple life in her village with the remainder of the money. Someone else said she would move to New York City and become a full-time writer (now, want to guess who this last one was??)

Fair to say that for all of these people, the only obstacle between them and their life dream is a financial one. Clearly.

Clearly?

Because if you want to be a writer, you can just write; if you want to take care of your family and friends there are lots of ways to do it that do not involve money; and if you want to make people feel good with your baking, well, just bake, yes? What stops you? I guess the apartment in Manhattan might take a little longer to secure… or not… who knows; and so we get discouraged, and we allow ourselves to forget to try, conveniently, because we think achieving the dream *just right* is not possible, not for us. And so, obviously, not even worth taking the first step toward it.

Instead we hit the sofa, we guzzle the beer, we fall asleep in front of the TV. And guess what, money's got nothing to do with it. We tell ourselves we cannot do what we want because we are too busy living, making a living, surviving… We pretend; we fake it.

You may have heard about Tommy Caldwell and Kevin Jorgeson, who a few months ago reached the summit of the 3,000-foot rock known as El Capitan in Yosemite National Park. They completed the first ever free ascent of the notoriously difficult section called the Dawn Wall. In fact, I heard another climber interviewed on TV say it was "impossible" to free climb it. But they did. For Caldwell this was the result of a seven-year obsession with the wall and this particular route.

Seven years: that is two-thousand five-hundred and fifty-five days…

Would that be plenty of time to ruminate on the dream not having been achieved *yet?* Plenty of time to doubt, to grow impatient, to hope and be disappointed, to study the route and shred his fingers on training climbs, to hope some more… to dare to believe? And maybe also to want to quit?

Because the easiest thing in the world is probably to give up on our dream; because it is too far, too complicated, too scary, too expensive, and much easier to convince ourselves that we do not care. Shrug it off and say it does not matter. Pass the bottle, please. Dream of the EuroMillions jackpot, the big enabler.

But what if we could? Then what?

I'll tell you a little story to illustrate this. After all, I am a trainer of NLP, and we like telling stories in NLP!

So, do you like sports cars? I do. I like old American ones especially. And so there was this Ford Mustang that travelled on the tracks with a bunch of trains. And the reason it stuck with the trains was that the Mustang's mother had abandoned it at birth – ran off with a BMW to travel Europe, of all things! Can you believe it?

And so the big heavy-haul goods train took pity on the little black mustang and raised it as one of her carriages. And on and on they went along the tracks, trudging along, always doing the same pattern.

And sometimes the little Mustang would look around as they went through the huge expanse of American wilderness, somewhere near highway 66 I think, and it would look, and look, and dream, of getting off the tracks, and of speeding down the highway toward freedom.

But trains do not work on the road you see. And even though the Ford Mustang had these weird little things underneath its body, round things with rubber on them, you know, the other carriages had always said, "Oh well, just ignore those – you look different, but you are one of us. We love you just the way you are."

And so the Ford Mustang just kept on dreaming, and dreaming, and dreaming, until one day it got so old that its wheels fell off.

I like this story. I guess if a Ford Mustang grew up thinking it was a heavy-haul goods train it would be worried about hitting the highway. Much better to stay on those tracks, right?

Get busy living…

Natalie Debrabandere
27 April 2015

PART ONE: LOSING MY MIND

On A Knife Edge

I cannot remember the exact date, and I guess it does not matter now, not really, but I know it was sometime in May 2011 that I found the knife.

I remember that night extremely well, like it has been seared against the inside of my brain. I was not working the next day, and I also was not training: preparation for an ultra-marathon, which I will go into a little bit later. So I thought it would be the perfect opportunity to unwind a little.

I had not planned to cut, had not even been thinking about it. As far as I was concerned the only thing that was going to happen that evening was that I was going to enjoy myself, for once. And what is wrong with enjoying yourself a little I wonder… Absolutely nothing, right?

How I had come to decide that I needed to let go and relax I do not recall either. Because I had been falling off the rails for quite some time, and the general consensus was that I was plenty loose in the head already. I had been slipping, big time, losing touch with my sanity. I certainly did not need to drink anymore, I did not need to get any more out of control than I already was… But it felt like so much pressure inside of me all the time!

Like everything was so hard and so much effort. I was so fed up with everything, and alcohol seemed like the perfect solution to blank it all out.

Being around other people was difficult, being alone was difficult, work was hard; I was lonely, tired, I wanted a break, and so that night I was going to do whatever I had to do in order to get it. I am nothing but determined, you know.

And was a little peace of mind really too much to ask? I was so tight and wound up I was almost vibrating with all the tension. I felt on the verge of exploding. And I did not know how to switch off, but I desperately needed to.

I was also back into proper training for an ultra-marathon at the time, and so since I had always been a runner, perhaps that was giving me an illusion of normality, and that it would really be okay to take my foot off the gas for at least one evening. It was a dangerous idea, I can see that now. But I was not thinking straight at the time and had not been for about a year and a half.

So I ordered a take-away from the local burger shop, and I bought two bottles of expensive red wine, just to be on the safe side. I was going to switch my brain off no matter what, and in those days just one bottle was never enough.

I sat on the floor, alone in my flat, eating my cheeseburger and drinking my wine, slowly, with the window open and the sun shining on my face, and for a little while I guess I managed to convince myself that it would be okay.

I was so very wrong.

Now like I mentioned previously, I was training for a fifty kilometre off-road race in Nottinghamshire, and the reason I was doing that was that I had recently been diagnosed with clinical depression. They said it was severe. It had been brewing for a while if you ask me.

In early 2010 I had spent five amazing weeks travelling the world with my (newly single) best friend. I say amazing because this was supposed to be "the trip of a lifetime", and in many ways it was.

I mean, who gets to fly in a helicopter and land on a glacier in New Zealand? Cross the Golden Gate Bridge on a Harley Davidson? Climb the Sydney Harbour Bridge and sea-kayak the beautiful waters of the Tasman Sea, amongst many other amazing adventures… But the thing is our friendship, our entire relationship was in trouble, and as we travelled through Australia, New Zealand and the US, I naively convinced myself that it was starting to improve.

I completely believed that we were in love and that we would get married once we got back to the UK. I knew I was in love, so much that it hurt. But love is not supposed to hurt, and obviously this should have been a sign that it was not right. Unfortunately it was completely lost on me. There had been loud warning bells everywhere along the way, but I had absolutely no idea that this trip was in fact a good-bye holiday, and that another woman was already waiting impatiently in the wings to take my place.

Talk about being blind. Talk about being stupid. Talk about denial.

When my friend told me that it was all over, the day after we landed back at Heathrow, I did not take it well, and that is the understatement of the century.

"Hell hath no fury like a woman scorned", you know the thing? Well, that was me, and then some. I was rage, fury and hurt all rolled into one. One big screaming ball of pain. I did not want to break up, no way, and I would not accept it. I felt incredibly let down, abandoned, used, scared, humiliated and angry. Oh boy, was I angry…

So angry in fact that the police had to warn me off. Stay away, they said, or things will get really bad for you. I had never, ever been in trouble with the police before, never so much as a parking ticket. All of a sudden, things in my life were unravelling at the speed of light, and I did not recognise myself. I could not understand my own reactions and emotions, and I could not stop the behaviour. I was completely out of control.

And I was also extremely unprepared for how quickly everything was happening. Change happens fast, I know that now. Whether we label it as positive or negative never makes a difference. And before I realised it, I was in big trouble, aka "severely clinically depressed."

Mind Stuff

So what is clinical depression? Well, according to the British NHS, it is more than simply "feeling unhappy or fed up for a few days."

Yep, I would say that is absolutely correct!

The NHS also say that depression is "a real illness with real symptoms, and it is not a sign of weakness or something you can "snap out of" by "pulling yourself together."

I do also agree with this, and I would suggest that the behaviour of being depressed happens in the absence of choice, which can be one of two things: either zero awareness of positive available options in response to a stressful event, the trigger if you will; or the cumulative effects of a bunch of limiting decisions, disempowering beliefs, and rules and the meanings ascribed to those, which have reduced our thinking to the size of a thimble and sucked all the resources out of our minds.

According to the World Health Organization, 350 million people worldwide suffer from depression. It is a leading cause of disability. The symptoms are as follows:

- extreme irritability over minor things
- anxiety and restlessness
- anger management issues
- loss of interest in favourite activities
- fixation on the past or on things that have gone wrong
- thoughts of death or suicide

Physical symptoms include:

- insomnia or sleeping too much
- debilitating fatigue
- increased or decreased appetite
- weight gain or weight loss
- difficulty concentrating or making decisions
- unexplained aches and pains

I was exhibiting and experiencing twelve out of the twelve symptoms listed above – and a few more for good measure, like high blood pressure.

A very good friend of mine, who was extremely worried about me, had suggested several times that I should go talk to someone. A "professional", she implied. It was obvious to her that I would never be able to get better on my own. Things were that bad.

In the UK, your GP (General Practitioner), would be your first port of call in this type of situation. I really did not like the idea of going to see mine; I did not "do" illness and doctors, you see, I never had. But my friend insisted, and so I relented. There was also that little twinkle of hope inside of me that maybe, just maybe, someone would be able to help me figure things out.

My GP was quite alarmed, horrified in fact, when I described what I was experiencing, and he decided to put me on Prozac immediately. He barely looked at me when he said that, and it only took about five seconds for him to make that decision; so then it was my turn to be shocked.

Prozac? Surely he was not being serious. I asked if there was anything else other than pills that I could do, and he waved me off with a vague mention of talking therapy, and a warning about six-months long waiting lists. Still not looking at me. In essence the message was clear: take the drugs I am offering you, and shut the hell up about it.

I am delighted to say that I took that box of pills, went straight home, flushed them down the toilet and resolved never to go see that guy again. I reasoned that I should have known what would happen anyway. That experience only reinforced my idea that GPs were useless, pills a total con, and I told my friend about it and asked her to please never mention it again.

Once again I insisted that I would get better, on my own, and on my own terms.

You know, my dad is a cyclist. And even when I was just about to be born, that was still no reason for him not to train. So he told my mum to wave a dish cloth out of the window if she needed him, and he went out to do thirty-two laps of a two-mile loop around the house, looking out for that dish cloth every time he pedalled past.

Hey, you know what, "obsessed" is a word the lazy use to describe the dedicated, so that's okay!

Maybe because of my father, certainly thanks to him in fact, I developed a real love for endurance sports; I really enjoy doing distance, whether it is in cycling or running. It is my thing, you see. And I love it that endurance is not entirely about muscles but even more about the mind.

I remember doing 100+k rides with my dad when I was fourteen or fifteen years old, and feeling fantastic; and going away to races, staying at cool little hotels in small towns in the French Alps, throwing up my lunch on one particularly hard climb, and being so cold on the descent of the Col du Galibier that I could barely flex my fingers on the brakes.

It was hard and it was beautiful. I loved the toughness of it and the feeling of achievement that I got from it.

Throughout it all, what my father's passion gave me was an opportunity to get acquainted with the power of my own mind. It was strong, and so was I. So when my mind let me down, it was a monumental shock. I did not know this sort of thing could happen, let alone to me, and I had absolutely no clue how to get myself back together.

You Won't Understand

In NLP (Neuro Linguistic Programming), we talk about the fact that "the map is not the territory."

What it means is that you can read someone a menu and tell them how great the food at your favourite restaurant is until you are blue in the face, but it still will not replace their experiencing the food first-hand.

The map is not the territory: you have to walk the trail or run the marathon before you can understand what it is really like. Until you do, maybe it also means that it would be wise to reserve judgment on what other people are going through in life. People are unique and we all experience things differently…

And that is a lesson I had to learn the hard way!

Obviously I have been doing NLP for a bunch of years now, and of course as a result I understand people a lot better, I understand how they think, and how this is turn shapes their behaviours. As a result I am a lot more tolerant in my judgement of others. A lot more "human" I guess. I understand now that people always do the best they can with the resources they have available at the time.

Also, my personal experience of depression and a nervous breakdown have certainly contributed to the building of a healthy dose of respect, and empathy, for the people around me in general and especially those who may be going through some difficult stuff. And my relationships have improved tremendously as a result.

This being said, for most of the earlier part of my life, I was absolutely ruthless in my opinions of others. I hated sick people, for example. I would go to them and bark, "Hey, what's wrong with you? Don't be sick! You are pathetic!" As if it was their fault of course! When I started working and people in the office were complaining of being stressed, I would say the exact same thing to them: "Shut up moaning and just get on with it, there is no such thing as stress!"

I was such a nice, warm-hearted little person, right?!

I was extremely sorry that I was a girl, a woman, because honestly, I thought it would have been really great if I could have become a Royal Marine. "Cheerfulness in the face of adversity" for example, one of their famous motto, is something that I was trying very hard to emulate in my own personal life.

I was into triathlon and distance running, I was doing rock climbing and sea-kayaking, riding a big motorbike and sky-diving; I was tough and I was in complete control of my mind and of my results. I did not know the meaning of failure. And I thought the most pathetic losers in the world were the people who said they "suffered" from depression.

"Just go for a run and you'll feel better," I would say to them, cold and unflinching. I did not do sick, I did not do unfit, I did not do out of control. But then it touched me... And I had no defence against it.

You know what, the map is not the territory.

So how dare that doctor, specialist, whatever he called himself, just throw me a bunch of pills and declare I needed taking care of? How dare he say to me, "If this does not work, we will have to consider a stay at a private clinic." What??

I thought, No way, this is not happening. That is just not me!

To be honest I got seriously scared then, and I remember vividly that for a couple of hours after my visit to that GP, things miraculously looked like they would start to improve. I was shocked into wellness again! Mainly I was outraged and completely bowled over by what that guy had said to me. I did not have depression and I did not need to go to some bloody clinic!

Clearly the man was insane, and boy isn't it ironic that I thought he was the one with the problem! But I decided to stay well away from drugs and well away from doctors in general, and indeed I stuck to my decision; I consider that it was one of the small personal victories of that time for me.

Unfortunately, it was the last one that I would get.

So instead of going on anti-depressants, I decided that I would run an ultra-marathon. Desperate times call for desperate measures I guess, so there we go! I was an experienced runner, I had several marathons under my belt already, and so I thought that it would be the perfect thing for me. It was a world that I knew and where I felt comfortable.

Perhaps naively, I thought that if I could finish that race and get my medal, that it would make me happy and that I would be cured of the depression that had taken hold of me. Yes, it would really be that simple. I would do what I told other people to do, follow my own advice, and just "go for a run."

Krissy Moehl, a very successful American ultra-marathon runner, was famously quoted once as saying that, "You can solve anything while out on a run, sometimes the run just has to be a little longer…"

So, fine; I could run, no problem. And I was hoping that the training would help too; training hard in the past always used to make me feel great, invincible, on top of the world, so hopefully it would have the same effect this time. I threw myself into it as if my life depended on it, and in a strange sort of way, it really did.

I did it my way, the hard way.

I was running or cycling every day, and doing back-to-back

long runs at the weekends; twenty miles on a Saturday, twenty-miles the next day, hammering it, trying to silence the sadness and the terror inside. Trying to deal with the anger. I knew that if I stopped and gave the depression a chance to catch up, that it would swallow me whole. I would have drowned in it, I knew that for sure.

Because even though I did not "believe" in mental illness, even though I so desperately did not want to accept that it was really affecting me, I was aware that something seriously weird was going on.

Going Dark

On top of all the other symptoms I was experiencing that clearly pointed to a major depressive disorder, my world suddenly got darker too; and this is not just a cute metaphor to say that I was depressed. Things went dim, literally. You know those dimmer switches you get in your home? It was exactly like that. The colours faded out.

I would go for long runs on beautiful sunny mornings, and everything looked grey. It was strange, because I had always enjoyed and appreciated being in nature before. As a child and throughout my adult life, in the summers especially, the colours always appeared so vibrant, so brilliant and so beautiful to me. Sometimes I would stand on top of a hill and look around me and almost be moved to tears by the beauty of it all. I was at one with my world.

But now, all of a sudden, I could not access any of those happy feelings, none of that connection. I had no idea what was happening at the time of course, although now I guess it is a great example of how much impact the thoughts you hold on the inside can have on the outside. The world out there had not changed per se, but I was definitely seeing it differently, perceiving it differently.

A team of neuropsychiatrists from the University of Freiburg in Germany recently highlighted this little known fact in one of their studies:

> "The processing of visual information related to contrast is altered in the retinae of depressed patients. A likely consequence of this is a reduced ability to perceive contrast – depressed people may indeed experience the world as being less colourful."

The study also indicated that the more seriously depressed people experienced the greater reduction in contrast gain.

Well, that is interesting to know now, but at the time I was not digging into scientific studies to try to understand what I was going through. I did not care about the science, I did not even know that some people were studying all this stuff. I did not define what was happening to me as a happy, interesting or valuable experience, or an opportunity to learn any lessons.

As far as I was concerned something was very, very wrong, and I was very, very scared.

I was also convinced that I could not afford to tell anyone what was really going on; the mention of a stay at a mental clinic was still fresh in my mind, and there was no way I was going to allow anyone to lock me up and put me on medication.

So I kept on running.

Now, on the other side of all of my NLP trainings, I

understand that I could have done things differently of course. I could have dissociated a little, reflected on my experience, and learned from it. I could have made it a lot less painful and learned what I had to learn from it a lot more quickly. But I could not access the necessary resources to do that at the time.

Nowadays I also understand that something does not have to be "real", the way that we define it, solid, in order for me to experience it. After all, the world and everything in it including our bodies is 99.999% empty space, so what the hell is real anyway, right? Basically, whatever I imagine, create and manifest in my life I will experience as real. That's the way it is, that is the way it works.

In my life today I know how to use this to my advantage of course; I create good stuff! But then I was lost. And believe you me, it was very real to me that night, after I had drunk a full bottle of red and was halfway through my second one.

So there I was about to discover self-harming for the first time.

It was nearly one o'clock in the morning, and Rocky was on TV. I remember it made me cry. I was staggering around the flat, looking out the window, back at the TV, unable to sleep and incredibly pissed off that I would run out of wine soon. Should have got more, I remember thinking, as if two bottles of heavy Chilean red were not enough.

I do not remember reaching for the knife, or even how I got the idea to do it in the first place; but I do remember standing over the kitchen sink with a big butcher's knife in my right hand, slowly dragging lines across the back of my left hand, watching intently as thick red blood mixed with tears slowly dripped off the blade. It gave me relief so incredible I could have done it forever.

It was the best feeling in the world.

Losing Touch

Since then many people have wanted to know why. Why in the world would I want to hurt myself like this, when I was already feeling horrible anyway?

Well, I started to cut because I was feeling like a pressure cooker; I was not inside one, I had become one, literally. The feelings of pain, sadness, rage, hurt and fear were all around me, and not just inside my head, but everywhere else inside every cell of my body as well.

As a result, cutting felt like the only way to let the pressure out, and thank God I managed to find a way that night, because I do not know what would have happened to me otherwise. I might have exploded, who knows.

Reaching for the knife felt very natural and logical to me at the time. There was no need to stop, or think, or analyse what I was doing. There was no guilt. I just knew somewhere deep inside myself that it was just the right thing to do. It made absolute perfect sense.

And for me it was a way of coping, not a way of punishing myself, like some people have suggested. It was not a cry for help, it was not a suicide attempt. Just the opposite in fact: it was the only way that I could find to carry on living.

I was careful with it too. I never cut too deep, and I never went at it for too long. I just did it until my hand felt like ice and it became difficult to move my fingers. Then, for a little while at least, I knew that I would feel peace. That peace of mind that I craved so much. The cuts would hurt nicely and the back of my hand would bruise and swell up. Most of the times I would have to go to bed with a bandage around it. I would hold on to it as I drifted off slowly, and I would feel the heat rising through my hand, like pain being liberated…

Then and only then would I be able to sleep.

Sometimes when I woke up in the morning I would have no memory of what I had done the night before. It was only when I spotted blood on the sheets that I would remember; or when I moved my fingers, and they felt tight and sore, I would stare at the wound, remember what had been going on, and sigh a little. I started to wear jumpers with extra-long sleeves to hide the cuts. I did not want anyone to see, to know, to try to stop me.

Could I have coped differently? Hell, I don't know… At the time, I really do not think so.

Like I said, I had no resources, no options. I have done some research since then and read about other ways that I could have dealt with my feelings. I am told I could have done things like punching a pillow, eating a chili or waxing my legs. Or yelled in the car with the windows all rolled up. Well, I don't know about that; maybe.

Perhaps the people who write this stuff need to experience the territory before they offer an opinion.

Anyway, that is what was going on for me that night in 2011. Drinking, and cutting, and going completely off the tracks, all the while trying to make myself feel better, the only misguided way that I knew how.

Oh, I completely aced that ultra marathon by the way, went home after it, downed a bottle of red and cried my eyes out. Now what? I thought. I felt nothing.

Toward the end of 2012 I was cutting still, whenever I needed to, which was often; I was also driving around after drinking too much, since alcohol had stopped having an effect on me, and as if things were not bad enough already, the company I was working for was undergoing a restructure, and my job was being made redundant.

I started to believe I would lose absolutely everything, that I would probably end up living on the streets, and also probably end up dead at some point.

The end was getting closer.

The only friend I had left, the one who had told me many times that I should go see a doctor, get help, the one who had cared about me way past the point when everybody else had run away, decided that she needed to take a break from me for a while too. I was scaring her with my crazy behaviour, and she was very afraid of what was in my future. She refused to be a part of what was to come.

So what did I do? You guessed it, nothing. I just thought, "Well, who needs you anyway?" and that was the end of it.

Now in retrospect, I am extremely grateful to her, and I am also extremely pleased to say that we are friends again. The reason I am grateful was that she had become my secondary gain (see definitions), and that is probably the single biggest obstacle to wanting to change.

Not wanting to "want to change", but really desiring to be different, with every fiber of your being. You see, my friend really did care about me. She gave me time. We went walking together, she cooked for me, we went for lunch in lovely little pubs, and chatted for hours – I was feeling loved and cared for, and I did not want that to change. I was not consciously aware of it of course, but this was definitely one important side-effect of my depression that was positive for me.

I am so happy that my friend made the decision to let go, because eventually a few months later this would mean that there would be absolutely no reason for me not to change. Finally, I had nothing left to lose; I had reached rock bottom and ground zero.

It was the best thing that could have happened to me and it is easy to see that in hindsight, but at the time it was awful.

I did not think it was possible, but I hardened a little bit more inside, contracted a little bit more. I convinced myself that I did not need her, or anyone else for that matter, and if I was going to be alone for the rest of my life it was perfectly fine.

I hit another low.

Out Of Whack

I told you about losing my colours, right? Well, something else had started to happen as well around that time, something extremely weird. As if it was not plenty weird already, you might say. But yes, it did get a little bit crazier, and if I had been scared before, this was on a completely new level of panic.

It seems appropriate to mention at this point that I am a huge fan of Patricia Cornwell, the best-selling crime writer, author of the famous Scarpetta series and the inventor of the Forensics/CSI genre. I keep up to date with her books and what she does on the side, and a little while ago I saw a video of a keynote speech she gave in front of staff at the McLean Hospital in Boston.

The hospital is dedicated to improving the lives of people and families affected by psychiatric illness.

In her address, Patricia briefly talked about how she manages her own bipolar condition (see definitions), and she said it is weird how sometimes people can spend hours and hours obsessing, ruminating, and wondering why they are feeling so bad for no obvious reason, when it is normally just "because their internal weather system is a little out of whack".

What Patricia is talking about is what we call "state" in NLP.

If I think of my state as an internal weather system, it makes it much easier for me to understand how fragile it could be, and how quickly it could change. And also how much of an impact the thoughts I choose to think can have on it. If your state is a weather system, then your thoughts are its jet stream.

Today I say, "Choose your thoughts with care, guys!"

I understand that it is always a matter of choice. Yes it is. We are in charge, we decide, and I get that now, no problem. But at the time I did not have a clue about all this stuff. I was in the middle of a hurricane, hanging on for dear life, and all of the theory was lost on me.

When you are okay and you feel good it all seems so normal, doesn't it? In NLP, we say a person's state is simply how they feel internally. No big deal, right? The word sounds rather dull and boring and like it would not matter much… and yet when our state is not right, when it is "a little out of whack" as Patricia would say, it can affect not only our capabilities but also the way that we interpret our experience.

And as I found out for myself, it is frighteningly easy to mess up your perception of the world, without even trying to.

When I was going through all of those traumatic events, I was feeling a little like I was made of crystal, and would shatter into a million pieces at the slightest touch. No wonder I started to lose it then.

Repeated exposure to constant, overwhelming anxiety or an early traumatic event, can cause you to step out of your own self. It is called Depersonalisation. The only specialist clinic for depersonalisation in the UK is based at The Maudsley Hospital in London. They state that "under intense trauma, becoming detached from one's body may seem a useful means of coping, but in some people, the depersonalisation then may become autonomous and a chronic disorder."

You can say that again. And this is exactly what I was experiencing, although true to form, I did not know what it was, what it was called, or how to deal with it.

There I was, stumbling around on the outside of my own life, wondering who had shaken up the pieces of my world and forgotten to put them back where they belonged. Honestly, I was screaming inside, yet nobody could hear. It was like being in an episode of the Twilight Zone, and you know what, maybe I was. Right there in no man's land, stuck by the side of the track that used to be my life. I had come off it, fallen off big time.

I was feeling very floaty inside, unattached and drifting, as I observed myself, my life and all around me from afar, knowing that I was getting further and further away with every passing day, not knowing how to stop or how to get back. If you had asked me then to describe what it was like, I would not even have been able to tell you, not really.

It was just a very powerful feeling, that is all. It was that sense of absolute detachment and complete inner serenity, and at the same time it was like being ejected out into outer space, gasping for air, scared out of my mind.

Pretty much, it was like watching myself slowly drift into madness. I started to think that I would not be around to see the start of 2013. I started to think that maybe I should get busy dying.

Suicide Anyone?

"There is a new app out there which will notify Twitter users if people they follow appear to be suicidal. The app uses an algorithm to identify key words and phrases which indicate distress. Those include "tired of being alone", "hate myself", "depressed", "help me" and "need someone to talk to." However it does not yet identify sarcasm, according to the website." (BBC News, 2014)

Here you go, folks, Twitter to the rescue! Oops, sorry, is that sarcasm?

If you enjoy philosophy, like I do (I am French after all!), I think there would be several solid starting points for discussion in the few lines above.

For now I would like to focus on just one, and that is this incredible obsession we all seem to have with breaking people down into minuscule criteria, to use rules and "algorithms" in order to label them as something that we can work with.

Might not be good for them, but hey, never mind. Then we can grab hold of them, keep a firm grip on them, and "really know them." Only then will other people no longer be scary, strange or difficult. Anyone who does not fit inside a box, with a few labels stuck to their forehead and the appropriate assortment of pills, should be viewed with suspicion it seems.

Some people hate not being able to stick a label on you, have you noticed? Now if you happen to change, if you happen to grow, and evolve, they will be quick to remind you: "Well, you used to hate spinach when you were three… and now twenty years down the line you are a vegan?? Surely you cannot be trusted."

Some people find it so difficult when you change.

Well, be slippery, I say! Change! Change often! Change faster than anyone can label you, and if you really have to put a label on yourself then make sure it is not one that limits you and keeps you stuck. Because the problem with labels is that when you start to identify with them, you actually become them, and then you stop moving.

When I was going off the rails, under the label of "clinically depressed", I did reach out to other people for help. I was only human after all, even though I considered not being able to handle what was happening to me on my own a weakness. I did not really know what I wanted, what I needed, but I think probably it was just a connection, or an anchor, any kind of support which would have been pretty wonderful in my situation.

Little did I know that what I really needed to do was to reconnect with my own self…

I have described how the depersonalisation was making me feel, like I was drifting further and further away from my body and my life. I think all I wanted at that time was for someone to notice me out there floating out toward emptiness.

I wanted for someone to grab my hand and hold on to me, to hold me back, to stop me leaving, because I sure as hell did not want to go where I was headed. I was terrified. I wanted someone to hug me and to say that it would be all right, I wanted someone to be there for me and make me feel better. (Notice the problem right there, by the way? *Someone else* to make me feel better…)

Anyway, I desperately needed someone to help. The need for other people at that time was irresistible, overwhelming, and yet I was all alone. Twitter did not fill that hole. And on that point, I hear people say all the time, "Oh, yes, Twitter is such a stupid thing; who needs to tweet about what they have eaten for dinner and that they're going to bed now and whatever? Who cares??"

Well, I can tell you from personal experience that sometimes sending a tweet out into outer space can make a person feel a little less lonely.

So late at night after a few drinks I would reach out and try to find help, on the phone and via email. Thankfully, there were "experts" and organisations out there who would be able to listen, maybe help me, and I would even be able to remain anonymous. It was almost as good as self-harming.

Almost…

On this subject, I think it is an amazing thing to work to save lives. Yet it seems that before we can help somebody, we first have to dissect their problem to such an extent that way too much energy is spent on it.

So, what have you got? Depression? Anxiety? Psychosis? Phobia? What is your label? Talk about it, tell me how it makes you feel. Oh, how I hated that part! It is like to get to the sky we first decide to dig all the way down to the centre of the Earth, and then turn around and climb back up.

Why don't we start flying straight away?

Perhaps it would be more useful to identify the opposite of the problem and dwell on that, to give that solution massive energy and potential, and teach the person tools and techniques to get to it?

Would that not be a million times better? Just sayin'.

Talking Ain't Helping

Sometimes by wanting to help someone, we can end up putting ideas in people's heads that may never have been there in the first place; or perhaps were there, but only as a lingering possibility that would never have seen the light of day anyway.

You know, there is a very fine, tiny little line between elicitation and installation. Throughout my "crazy years" as I call them now, I have had some experience of organisations that work to prevent suicide, and yet do it in such a clumsy way that they may end up planting the idea inside people's heads instead.

So listen, maybe it is late at night, you feel really sad, you are a little drunk and very lonely, and you are not just writing a country song, right? (Obviously, if you are, good for you!)

You know there is a number that you can call. The people on that number are not allowed to tell you to get lost, and they will not call the cops on you just because you are trying to get in touch. Win-win. Would it be a little bit tempting to ring up then? Well, I think so, yes. Massively! And I did do that a few times, although I stopped as soon as I realised what was happening.

Because when I got through, the person on the phone would start to ask a bunch of depressing questions like this: "Do you ever feel like you can't carry on?" "Do you ever feel like life is just too much?" "Have you ever thought about ending it all?"

I mean, come on! Mate, I am feeling really awful right now and all I want is someone to cheer me up, okay?!

I do not see the point of any of these questions, do you? I do not think asking anyone if they are suicidal is helpful. I do not think suggesting it to them is helpful either.

"Ending it all, well, no, I hadn't thought of that, but now that you mention it, thanks… Hey, is there an app for that?"

So maybe the caller have said a few "red alert" words. Maybe the thought has indeed crossed their mind, and maybe they are not even aware of it. Maybe they are. So what? What are you going to achieve by discussing it and dwelling on it? They are on the phone, aren't they? Right now. They might never call again, so right there and then could be our only opportunity to ask the lifesaving questions.

And there are some very powerful questions we could ask, questions that could mean the difference between someone sinking back into hard-core depression, or clicking into wanting to live again. And you know what, one click is all it takes. One.

We get told that change is hard and difficult, that it takes a long time, that you need lots and lots of pills and years of counselling before you can hope to feel better... if ever. Well, that is so not true! It is a bunch of lies!

Ewan Mochrie, international Master Trainer of NLP and CEO of Inspire 360, the UK's leading school of NLP training, wrote something in one of his articles that I would like to use again, because if I could only keep one thing from the work I did with my coach it would be this one:

"One thing that is often missed by practitioners in all talking therapy fields, is that fundamentally the patient or client doesn't actually need any 'technique' to change, they can just change."

How can I be so confident about that, you may ask. How do I know? Well let me tell you, I am hugely confident about it. Massively sure of myself! I know, like I know, like I know, that I am right. I know because I have done it.

I have done it guys, and so can you!

The problem is in what we choose to believe: do not believe the words of the people who have themselves been indoctrinated to believe in limitations and impossibilities. Choose to think differently, like I did.

Okay, let's picture the problem (depression, addiction, anything you want), as a square piece of dusty ground in the middle of the Arizona desert, with five-mile-high walls on all sides and yourself stuck in the middle – however you imagine your problem obviously, but this works well for me!

Ask yourself what would happen if you were able to fly up high above the walls, and drop down on the outside? And once you are there, what if you were able to take a real good look? To take a deep breath and expand a little? To gaze toward the mountains on the horizon and feel the warm gentle wind on the back of your neck, to listen to the sounds of the desert and marvel at the vastness of it all, to realise that there are no barriers, no limits, just complete and absolute freedom…

How good would that feel?

If you could get outside the walls and look back at your problem, would you see then that you have no problem?

Think about that for a minute.

Sometimes, "outside looking in" is a good place to be. I managed to get to that place, by choosing to think differently. And once I was there I had a simple choice to make, and I chose to get better. I chose to live. I realised, in a flash almost, that I did not have a problem. Never had in fact.

I took off that coat of sadness and depression, closed my eyes, turned my face to the sun, and threw my arms up in the air. I was free.

Solutions, not problems.

That is what NLP is all about. And there is no whinging allowed either, which I must admit pleases me no end! Of course I know that some people would prefer to just moan about their problems for hours on end and do nothing about it; secondary gain is a powerful motivator, I am aware of that. I did have some of it going on at one point as I explained earlier.

For a while I tried counselling, and to be honest it went something like this: sit down, moan about my life for an hour, hand over £50. Four weeks later: sit down, moan about my life for an hour, hand over £50. Nothing achieved, nothing changed.

I mean, it was good to moan I guess, sometimes, and sometimes it was good to have a good cry too, but I was looking for way more than that. I did not want to spend the rest of my life crying and complaining! I mean seriously: who would, right?

Solutions, not problems.

"Shit happens", as the bumper sticker goes... Life is offered to us black and white and tasteless, and it is our job to colour it and add flavour along the way. This is what it means to be human, and what an amazing opportunity it is!

Which colours we choose, whether we add salt and tears to our journey or chili flakes and a zest of excitement, is up to us and us only. And you know what, no wonder people so often build prisons instead of lives; we are encouraged and conditioned to do so from birth. We are taught to believe that we are helpless! We are taught to believe in limitations.

Well I say: ENOUGH!

What if there was another way? What if we already had all the resources we need, somewhere deep inside?

Let me tell you this: learning NLP did not make me want to kill myself. It did, however, completely destroy my problem. The effects associated with that are significant and should not be underestimated!

Here are a few of the things you might have to learn to live with if you choose to start to "Think NLP":

- Increased self-confidence
- The ability to see opportunity in adversity: better results
- Improved relationships with your colleagues, friends and family
- Your fears will disappear! Instead you will feel excited to try new things, to explore and to expand!

No kidding: these are all things that I have personally experienced.

You know, there are a few things I want to talk about in this book, and one of them, which I am extremely passionate about, is that it is up to each and every one of us to create the sort of world we really want to live in. And we can, we really can! We can create a world where people will want to be alive, to share, to love, and to thrive.

We have the power, we always did, and all we need now is to be reminded of it.

>We can be powerful beings…

>We can live amazing lives…

>We can be happy…

>We can change…

>We can do it…

>Be better…

<u>YOU CAN!</u>

Believe...

Probably the toughest ultra marathon in the world is Badwater, a 135-mile race from Badwater in Death Valley (282 feet below sea level) to Whitney Portals on Mt. Whitney (8360 feet).

During the race, at the deliciously named Furnace Creek, temperatures can get up to 135° Fahrenheit. And it is very common for runners to experience hallucinations.

Scott Jurek, who won the race twice, says on the Badwater website that "to ultra-runners hallucinations are like grass stains to Little Leaguers. Ultra-running is a sport stuffed with long stretches of agony."

He also explains that although he does not necessarily enjoy putting himself in such a place of hurt and pain, it is "one of the most transformational places to be mentally and physically. So when I'm out on the race course having a really tough time - that's usually when the breakthroughs happen."

I know exactly what Scott means. If I had not gone through three long years of hard-core depression and desperate self-harming, I probably would never have discovered NLP, and my true purpose in life. And so I really am incredibly grateful for these three years of perceived "hell", and all of my experiences.

Like many people out there, I have discovered that on the other side of the most unbearable challenge I thought I could face, there was an ocean of possibilities waiting for me. And when I discovered NLP, I found the paddle to go with my canoe. Now I can easily steer my way on the river of Life.

So what is this NLP thing, really?

Well, it is a life-saving tool, for one. An eye-opener, too. A light that you can use to slice through the fog of all the lies we are always being told about who we are, as human beings, and what we can really achieve if we get in touch with our inner resources and the power of our own mind.

Power and resources that we all have, but that we do not know that we have.

And you know what, I would not change a single thing about my journey so far. It has been perfect. It is perfect right now, all the time, even when it is not.

I chose to become a trainer of NLP in order to help other people become empowered. To help as many people as I can start to really believe in themselves. And take action on that too. Because the more people choose to think differently, the more people decide to challenge the limiting rules and beliefs we have created and that we live by, in ourselves and our society, the closer we can get to a better world. Heaven on Earth is a real possibility you know, we can make it happen!

Now here are a few examples, true stories, of people who choose to view the world a little differently and the big difference that it can make. Let's start with a cycling one in honour of my dad:

Robert Marchand is a French cyclist who recently broke his own hourly world record. Marchand rode 26.927 kilometres, 2.5km more than he did when he had just turned 100 years old, **two years ago**. "With doping I could have ridden faster," Marchand joked. "But there is no doping. I only have water with some honey in my bottle here."

Compare this with a recent article in the UK's Daily Mail:

"Turning 50? Time to start worrying. Rather than being an exciting milestone, many of us regard 50 as the age when we start to become anxious about getting old. A poll of Britons aged 50 and over found that eight in ten worry about getting older. And one in twenty of us start to fret about aging before we even reach 40."

Well, I guess it is a good thing that nobody told Robert! Or perhaps he chose not to listen?

But seriously, what would you rather choose to believe? That you can be a world champion at a hundred years old, or that you should start planning for your funeral when you turn fifty?

And would believing really make a difference, you might ask? Well, yes, I believe it would! In fact, I know it does, because I have tried it for myself; I use that thinking everyday in my life now, and I get amazing results.

Here is another example in case you need a little more convincing:

> At thirty-three years old, Steve Way was overweight and a twenty-a-day smoker. Seven years later he finished tenth in the marathon at the Commonwealth Games. He said "I **believed** there was a marathon runner in me waiting to get out."

There you go. 'Nuff said! And I guess he was too busy training hard to read the headlines about how turning forty was going to slow him down, too!

So what do you think? Of course you could decide that Robert and Steve are sporting anomalies, and dismiss them as regular impossibilities. This would be a belief you choose to have, and that is absolutely fine. Whatever works for you. But what would happen if… the world was not like we think it is? What if what we actually believe really could make a difference?

See what international author and peak performance strategist Tony Robbins has to say about that:

> "Beliefs have the power to create and the power to destroy. Human beings have the awesome ability to take

any experience of their lives and create a meaning that disempowers them or one that can literally save their lives."

Nice! Beliefs are so intangible, and yet they can have so much power!

I had a happy little moment a few years ago when I decided once and for all that really, it is fine that my entire life is kind of like a dream. Does not mean I do not take it seriously of course, but only to a degree. And here is why it is fun, and relevant to this conversation we are having.

I can be incredibly passionate about things, which is good obviously. Passion, spirit, drive, enthusiasm, all of these things are great. But I have lost track of the number of things, hobbies and people I fell in love with, only to wake up a week or so later, feeling nothing, wondering what on earth had possessed me to sign up for a new training course, book a flight, buy expensive kit, you name it. Like it had all been a dream.

Sometimes as a result of simply changing my mind about something, or believing differently, entire groups of people would vanish from my life, too. It was fine, but it was weird regardless. I used to bump into these people all the time, and now they are gone? Yet we still live in the same town, drive the same roads, shop in the same places… but we do not cross paths anymore.

What was going on? All I had done was change my mind…

For a few years, knowing I had this tendency to blow all hot and cold about stuff, whenever I decided to do something new I would always hesitate and say to myself, "Hang on a minute, is this real, or am I going to wake up tomorrow and discover this is just another illusion? Can I really trust myself here?"

Obviously I did not know for sure what the real thing would look like, but I had a sense that it might involve some kind of permanence. Surely some things could be counted on to stay the same, right?

I had this very dangerous belief that we should be able to protect the things that are really worth it and precious, like people and relationships; to keep them from change forever. If it stayed then it was real, if it was real then it would stay. And things had to be real, solid and permanent in my world.

Well, like I mentioned previously, the universe is mostly made out of empty space, of energy, and that includes our own physical selves. So the ideas of solidity and permanence really are strange ones to pin on the back of that one! Change is here to stay. What we choose to believe about it matters. And what we believe about the power of our own minds to create matter, to create our world, matters even more. So why not simply learn to take advantage of it, and have fun with it?

A New Reality

So, am I just making stuff up out of nothing? Probably, as we all are.

We do it by using what we call in NLP our "Model of the World": a collection of personal beliefs and values, the basic structure behind our reality construct. None of it is "real", it is just a tool we have to experience life on this planet.

So would it make sense that I can experience another kind of life, just by changing my model of the world? Oh yes! And that is awesome!

In my current model of the world, nothing is carved in stone and change is good and the only constant. And by being aware of the paradoxical core part of me that never moves, that is always there, that some people call their Higher Self and which is always solid and steady in the background, I can allow myself to experience change in complete safety. To enjoy it, to play with it, to explore, to do all I can do to bring more of it into my life. Because it really is all good.

What is right? What is real? I think we decide, don't we?

Maybe that is the whole point of being alive as well: to

enjoy it, to have as many adventures as possible, to explore! Let us not deny ourselves the wonderful opportunity that we all have, each and every second of our lives, to design our own experience. And what would be the point of creating a miserable one?

There is nobody out there holding the key to your destiny, who is going to greet you with a clipboard and a checklist one day. Your life is yours to live. You are free to change your mind, to reinvent yourself, as much and as often as you like. You can change, quickly, when you decide to, and there are no limits to what you can be, do, and have…

Talking about change, I was reading author Tim Freke's *The Mystery Experience* the other day, and one sentence stopped me in my tracks. Tim wrote that, "There is no death, just a transfer of attention."

Well, what an enchanting idea! Really, really attractive to me. Because death will be a big change all right, when I finally get to it one of these days, and I am incredibly curious about it. I am curious because I absolutely believe it is the start of something else. And we do not know where we go when we die. We know where our bodies go, but what about us? Where do we go?

French philosopher Pierre Teilhard de Chardin suggested that, "We are not human beings having a spiritual experience. We are spiritual beings having a human experience."

This means that we are not a body which happens to have a soul, we are souls which have chosen to spend a little bit of time inside of our physical bodies. Reflect on that for a minute, see how it makes you feel. Cool, right? Great idea... So what does it all mean?

Well, when I change my mind, my *focus*, and I notice that my outside world seems to be different, is it like a tiny transfer of attention taking place? Does something really happen, do I go somewhere else? Is it why those people I used to bump into all the time suddenly are not there anymore?

And if I go somewhere else, how many other places are there to explore? What would we call these places? Other lives? Different Models of the World? Parallel universes?

I choose to call them different realities.

Might not be as strange and impossible as people think, you know. We all look out there and we think that the world is what we can see, taste, hear, and touch, and yet this is only what our senses let us experience, so how do we know for sure?

If you think you know what is going on out there in the universe, I suggest researching some of the recent discoveries of Quantum Mechanics.

Here are a few examples taken from a great website called *theuniversesolved.com*:

- String theorists believe that our world consists of eleven dimensions (we can only perceive four at the moment: length, width, height and time.) As human beings we are incredibly limited by our senses.

  "Water? I have no idea what you're talking about, you must be mad!", says the fish.

- We get 2,000,000 bits of information hitting our brain every second, but we can only process approximately 134 bits per second: so frustrating!

  Think of all the stuff we are missing!

- IQOQI, the Austrian Academy of Sciences Institute for Quantum Optics and Quantum Information, has experimentally determined that objective reality does not exist to a certainty of 1 in 80 orders of magnitude.

- And what about this: maybe there is no time, and what we experience as time is in fact the feeling that we get from constantly shifting between parallel universes, aka different realities.

Okay, bring on the Twilight Zone theme tune!!

But guys, isn't all this stuff incredibly exciting?

Obviously you do not need to become a quantum physicist yourself in order to break out of depression. Phew! But just for a second, please allow yourself to consider that maybe we create our worlds, through our thoughts, values and beliefs. So let's create something wonderful, okay?

NLP is a tool that you can use to do exactly that. And to learn how to think differently, and open your mind to extraordinary ideas; to reframe limitations into possibilities; to blow up the barriers that keep us stuck inside tiny thinking patterns, and to understand, invite and embrace positive change. All this in order to construct many lives, many models, always evolving and inventing, always learning, shifting, exploring and growing – with complete volition, knowing deep down inside that it really is all good.

How does that sound? Great? Okay. I think I have spent enough time now hinting at what NLP can do, and what an amazing tool it is… So let's drill down a little deeper and find out what NLP really is all about, shall we?

Odd Is The New Normal

I went to a national NLP conference recently, and it is fair to say that it was very cool to be amongst like-minded people for once.

Normally when I say NLP, most people do not know what I am on about, or they are scared of it; but at the conference that night, there was no need to explain, no need to try to convince people that it is not mind control, no need to answer questions about whether or not I can tell someone is lying just by watching their eyes...

It was nice to be able to relax. Meet some friends. And talk philosophy at the dinner table. Awesome!

Tim Freke, the wonderful author I mentioned previously was there too, and it was great to watch him present. In the book I quoted from earlier, *The Mystery Experience*, Tim reflects that, "We act as if we understand what it is to be a human being, when actually it is an enormous enigma of mind-boggling proportions."

I love it that I got to meet people at the conference who are not afraid to think odd thoughts about who we are and where we come from. I like having my mind boggled. Because really, who is to say odd things are not the truth behind the pretend?

I think sometimes other people are odd, you know…

Recently, someone told me that if I was interested in learning about the history of religions, the only book I needed to read was the Bible. "Don't bother with anything else," they said, "it is all in there. And it is THE TRUTH."

When I showed her my pendulum, just for fun, that woman was seriously worried that I was part of some kind of cult! I will not tell her that there was a Bible in my hotel room at the conference, and that I was too busy having fun and discussing the Intervention Theory with a fellow odd person to pay any attention to it…

The thing is though, you do have to be a little bit careful with beliefs. It is very easy to decide on a belief, something that fits your current thinking and facilitates your experience, and to latch on to it really hard and reject anyone who thinks differently and challenges your thinking.

With that in mind, who is to say that what I believe is right anyway?

Well, I guess a good way of measuring the validity of my beliefs would be by the results that I get. I am no longer depressed – actually, let me rephrase this: I no longer choose to do the behaviour of depression. Much better. Also, I do not self-harm anymore. I have become aware of my own power to choose to do things differently.

When I started doing NLP trainings I had no idea that my end goal would turn out to become just one of many along the way. Becoming a practitioner turned out to be the key to another dimension, a new reality: so there really is a reason behind the reason! And a world behind this world. And a truth behind what everyone else has told me up until this point! Wow!

I became aware of this curtain in front and all around me. Previously the curtain had been invisible, but now I could see it, and I could slip on to the other side. Over there life was brighter, happier, full of potential, easier and successful. All of a sudden, I was thinking there just is not enough time for me to learn everything I want to learn, and so I guess it is a good thing that linear time is just an illusion!

Oh yes: really.

I get people all the time telling me they cannot change because of their past. They believe that their past has made them into the person they are today, and that they cannot change the direction they are going in. **But what if you could change your past, by changing your present?**

Take me for example: do you think the way I live my life now, the person that I am today, was created from the experience of folding and breaking when I got hit with a little bit of difficult emotional stuff? Of course not.

Although there is a reality in which I am still depressed and self-harming, probably. There is also a reality in which I ended up getting married to my best friend after we came back from our travels. And of course there is a reality in which we never even met. Endless possibilities, all co-existing together, *at the same time.*

Now, because of what I choose to do in the present moment, the only one where I am able to impact anything, I influence not only my future, but also my past. In the past of the present I am living now, what I went through did not break me: it made me.

So do you see how by choosing to be different in the present moment you could also reshape your past and put yourself in the reality of the person you really want to be?

Do you think this is odd? Well, when you start to read the theories of modern quantum physics you will realise that it makes perfect sense. And that is hard science I am talking about folks.

You know, maybe "odd" is not that odd after all. People lie all the time, don't they? They tell you that Santa is real, and that they did not have sex with that woman, but we know better, don't we! People also say you cannot have everything you want in life, and I think the speakers at the NLP conference that I went to would disagree with that.

I would certainly disagree with that.

You can have everything you want in life, the question is, are you willing to shift your thinking? Because this stuff is tried and tested, and I can absolutely guarantee that your life will change if you do.

In NLP, we understand that our words do not describe the world that we live in, but rather that they **determine** the world we live in. As human beings, we are used to think that the world is made of solid stuff, and yet our thoughts are like ripples of energy on the structure of the universe.

They matter a hell of a lot because they end up being solid things eventually. Don't they?

Well, how did we create the Jumbo Jet?

We imagined it, we thought it into existence. We did not think of it and then decide not to make it happen because we were scared. Or because we chose to believe we were not good enough. Or smart enough. We simply dreamed of it, made a plan, took huge amounts of action, and got the result that we wanted.

Think of this book you are reading. It is the same thing: I thought it into existence.

After I did NLP for the first time, my coach asked me how I felt about the whole thing, and my answer was that I felt like I had been given permission to change. I think more people need to do that. Give themselves permission to be, do and have all that they can.

So, back to NLP.

It really amuses me that I had to wait until I was about half-way through my Master Practitioner certification before I was able to explain properly what NLP is! There is a little bit of jargon going on.

If you want an easy get out of jail one-liner, you could say that NLP is a study of excellence, and a model of how individuals structure their experience.

If you want to use the words of Gina Mollicone-Long, who wrote the amazing book *Think Or Sink*, you could say it is internal change for external results. If you want to go a little bit deeper into it you could say this:

NLP is a synthesis of Cognitive and Behavioral Psychology. It stands for:

- Neuro: The nervous system through which our experience is processed via five senses: Visual, Auditory, Kinesthetic, Olfactory, Gustatory.

- Linguistic: Language and other nonverbal communication systems through which our neural representations are coded, ordered and given meaning. Includes: pictures, sounds, feelings, tastes, smells, words (Self Talk).

- Programming: The ability to discover and utilize the programs that we run (our communication to ourselves and others) in our neurological systems to achieve our specific and desired outcomes.

Oh come on… what is NLP really???

Okay, try this:

- NLP is how to use the language of the mind to consistently achieve your specific and desired outcomes.

- NLP is the study of human experience, communication, thinking, language and behaviour.

- NLP is about noticing conscious and unconscious behavioural patterns. It is about modelling excellence and understanding the process in how we communicate to ourselves and others (Thank you, *inspire360.co.uk* for the above definitions)

At the core, that is what NLP is: a simple tool to empower yourself.

When you have the tool, the rest is up to you. You could do anything, really.

I chose to become a trainer and write a book: not bad for someone who thought she would not live long enough to see forty, right?

PART TWO: NLP NITTY GRITTY

My Experience As A Client

I discovered NLP just before Christmas 2012.

I was online one night and ended up googling counselling. I had done counselling before, and as you know it had been a complete waste of time, not solutions-focused enough for me. I certainly did not want to try any of that again, but maybe it was my unconscious mind telling my fingers to do the walking on that occasion. Trying to save me.

And so I ended up seeing that name pop up, a name that I thought I recognised, and I clicked on it and realised that the woman I had heard about for her record-breaking long distance swims around the world was a counsellor. A coach, she called herself. A coach of NLP. And she lived in my home town a five minute drive away from me. It sounded promising.

So I immediately thought, this is great: I am into distance running, she does distance swimming, hey, we must be kindred spirits.

I decided I would feel comfortable talking to her. What if

she could help me? All of a sudden a little bit of hope got reawakened inside of me. And yes, the coaching sessions were a little bit on the expensive side, but I thought you know what, if I am not going to be around in 2013, who cares about that anyway, so let's go for it.

On that note: obviously, I did stick around for 2013, and beyond! I am in love with my life right now! I love being alive, I love living. I am not kidding when I say that I get up every morning feeling incredibly excited about the day ahead. And so at the end of 2013 not only was I still there, alive and kicking, but I had an entirely new kind of problem on my hands: would I do NLP Master Practitioner training, or would I study to become a helicopter pilot instead? You could say that I was thinking a little bit differently all of a sudden, right!?

I was thinking in possibilities.

So how did that shift happen, and what was it like to experience NLP as a client? Well, this is an interesting story, and I am very happy to be able to share it with you.

When I went to see my coach for the first time, (her name is Julie by the way) she pointed to a broken piece of pine board on the floor in front of her TV, and she declared, "See that board? This is where I want you to leave your conscious mind. I am only interested in talking to your Unconscious Mind."

I immediately thought, "Wow, that's good... Different! I have no idea what it means, but that's good!"

It was definitely not like your bog-standard counselling session, exactly what I had been looking for, and so we were off to a great start. Although I also started to worry a little bit then, because I was wondering, "What if I haven't got one of those? What if I haven't got an Unconscious Mind??"

As you can see, I had some learning to do!

Need to tell you as well that now I feel very proud to also have a broken piece of pine at home, my very own, that I broke as part of an exercise on my Master Practitioner training. Some people do fire-walking, we did board breaking, and it was awesome. Amongst other things, breaking the board is a great metaphor for breaking through whatever you believe is holding you back in life. I had a lot of fun doing it!

So anyway, I sat there with Julie, she asked me a few questions about myself and what had been going on in my life, and she said we could do some Time Line Therapy™ if I wanted to (see definitions); and I said, "Yeah, sure, why not?"

Again, no idea what it was, but this was my last chance, you see. I would have done anything to bring some positive change into my life. It was either that, or dying.

So my coach guided me through the process for identifying my time line, and I remember having this weird conversation about what mine looked like at the time, which always makes fellow NLP people laugh.

"My time line looks like an American road, is that okay?" I said, worried.
Julie replied, "Great!"
And I insisted, "You know, it's got that yellow line like they've got on the side in the US, is that okay? Is that normal?"
She smiled and she said, "Yes, dear, it's wonderful."

When she told me we were going to have a "test flight" above the time line, I literally thought she was going to start hovering. I was so into it! I was so primed for RESULTS! I was probably the best client an NLP coach could ever want!

I think she probably guessed what I was thinking from my expression, because she cautioned, "For now we will just have to imagine it, all right? I have not mastered the art of flying around the house... yet..."

These NLP people do talk funny sometimes. Although I still think that Julie can fly, but hey, that's just me!

Another thing that she did was very bizarre – she talked at me, that's right *at* me, and it did not make any sense.

Now, I am very AD, which does not stand for Attention Deficit in NLP, but for Auditory Digital. Some people are very visual, others are very tactile, I am very AD. Meaning that I make sense of things inside my head; I analyse things; I have a lot of self talk; I compute meanings. The technique that my coach used with me that day is great for AD people.

The results were quite interesting to say the least:

a) it literally made my brain swim, and

b) well, and some of you might know this about me, I am originally from Marseille in the South of France. So English is not my first language. Up until that point I had always thought that my English was excellent, although this coach of NLP started to make me think that I was losing it – my English, I mean.

Because she would say something to me, and first of all, that was strange in itself because she said she was going to ask me a question, but she did not want me to answer it. She said, "I don't really want you to answer me, I just want you to really consider it."

And then she would speak a series of words that all made perfect sense individually, but not together. It was difficult trying to make enough sense out of the sentence, let alone "consider" anything… It was very unsettling. But I was determined to give it my best.

And so Julie would say a bunch of words, my eyes would go all the way around my head a couple of times, then the other way, I would frown and think really hard, and then I would ask, "Uh, say again please?" And she would burst out laughing, looking delighted, as if that was the joke of the century and go, "Sure! No problem!"

I was thinking this NLP thing was just absolutely bonkers. And that woman was clearly mad.

Little did I know at the time that the technique she was using so expertly is taught on the Master Practitioner programme! And so when I realised that I just knew I had to get myself on it and learn everything about it.

If you remember, I talked about the way I imagined my problem earlier, as a patch of ground in the middle of the Arizona desert surrounded by high walls: well, this was not simply a metaphor. In fact, the technique I went on to learn is the one that will allow you to fly high up above the walls of any problem, and leave it behind.

I decided right there and then that helicopter training would simply have to wait!

I Can Just Change!

That very first session I had with my coach lasted about two hours, and I walked out of there with my brain on fire, feeling slightly disconcerted, and with a couple of tasks to get completed before our next session. I was hopeful that this was the beginning of happier times, and a new way of looking at life.

NLP Coaching is all about tasking by the way, and taking action. Because nothing will ever change unless you take action, unless you do something about it, it is vital that you go and do the tasks, even if you think it is hard, or boring, or you cannot really understand the reason behind it.

This is something I tell all my clients: you have to do it!

As it was, I had no problems with my particular tasks.

    1 – I was asked to go away and write something that started with: "Now that I no longer have my problem,…" and basically write about the sort of life that I was having then. This is a great little exercise, and if you ever want to give it a try by the way, here is a little tip: write it in the present tense, as if it is already happening.

    2 – My coach gave me a copy of *The Secret* DVD and

asked me to watch it. I am sure a lot of you will be familiar with it, but I had not heard of it at the time, and when I first put it on it made me cry. It was tears of joy. Somehow I had always known this is the way it works, and now all of a sudden it was like I was being given permission to think that way. Again, being given permission: like being let out of jail. The feeling of relief I got was indescribable, it was a massive weight off my shoulders.

3 – Julie also gave me a copy of Gina Mollicone-Long's book, this one called *The Secret Of Successful Failing,* to read.
Now, I remember telling her in no uncertain terms at that point that if I ended up losing my job, and my flat, and landing on the street, it would be a huge failure, a massive disaster, and there would be no success in it whatsoever!

But never mind: I read the book and watched the DVD, I wrote (a lot) about the life of my dreams I was having without my problem, and the lights came on and things started to click into place. I started to see things differently. Specifically, I understood that the book was about the fact that there is no failure in life, only feedback.

You see, if you decide that you have failed, then there is nowhere to go from it, right? You failed, bummer, oh well, forget about it then.

But if you understand that all there is in reality is feedback, then you can be grateful about the information you have received, because every single bit of it that you get will help you reach your final destination.

Adjust, tweak, re-think, do it again, differently, get more feedback and be grateful for it, and just KEEP GOING.

So for me, things started to make sense at last.

One of the things I have learnt to do with NLP as well is how to take a step back; take a deep breath; look at it again, whatever "It" is. The situation I am in, the challenge, the obstacle, the opportunity, whatever. Now I can see the patterns instead of getting lost in all the little details. And I try to stay a bit loose and fluid in my thinking too, just to give things a chance to happen.

So if you are reading this book you are reading it for a reason, and maybe it is not so obvious exactly what that reason is right now. And perhaps there are things that have happened to you throughout your life so far that you chose to discard as funny little coincidences. And maybe if you take a step back and look at the messages hidden in the patterns, it might tell you something about the path that you are on right now.

The devil is in the detail, and way up high above the trees is where the magic happens.

You know, sometimes it pays to have tunnel vision. When I took my motorbike test only a few years after settling in the UK, I had tunnel vision. You could say I was "in the zone", focused, hyper-alert, even a nuclear blast would not have been enough to penetrate my concentration. That was good.

Sometimes though we get tunnel vision because we are stressed, anxious, or scared. Or depressed. We contract. We can see nothing but the problem, the brick wall in front of us.

When I was standing on that piece of desert behind the walls, deep inside my problem, I had no vision. Of course not, and no one in the same position would. The thing is we do it to ourselves. We become prisoners of our own thoughts, and our awareness contracts into total blindness.

We can see, feel and hear nothing but our problem. We cannot think outside the boundaries, not up, not sideways, not underneath. The solution might literally be standing right in front of us, waving and shouting at us to notice it, but as long as we are in our tunnel vision state we will not have any idea that it is there.

What I would say to you if that is the case for you right now is take a step back, come out of yourself a little, and become the observer of your own life for a moment. Let go of the situation, let go of the feelings, let go of the little details. Elevate yourself above all this and have a look at the structure.

"You" are not your current life situation. In any given moment you are always much more than that.

This "you" that I am talking about is the part of me that was leaving me at the time when I was experiencing depersonalisation. It is your core, the part of you that is eternal, that goes on existing even after your physical body dies. And, like the unconscious mind, we all have one.

Your Higher Self does not really care if you are losing your job, if your relationship is on the rocks, or whatever else you have chosen to label as "bad". Instead, your Higher Self is simply content to observe. It assigns no meaning to anything. It simply is.

Now that I have managed to reconnect with this very precious part of myself, it is a tremendous source of peace. It keeps me grounded. I know that I can involve myself fully in the day to day nitty-gritty of my life, and yet when things become a little bit stressful or difficult I know that I can get in touch with my Higher Self, and get settled again. I believe this is the whole point of meditation by the way, to get reconnected with the source.

Everything is always good, everything always comes just when you need it, in the way that you need it most.

So whenever you feel yourself getting way too tangled up in the intricacies of your current life situation, when you start to really struggle with the events in your life and the meanings that you assign to them, if you feel yourself going a little crazy, get in touch with your Higher Self too, be still for a moment, reconnect, take a bit of distance, and observe what is going on.

Solutions are many and plentiful, if only we decide to really look for them. If we allow ourselves to connect with them.

The Science Of Excellence

In total I had about five hours of work with my coach, spread over two sessions, with some very clever and effective tasking in between. Yes, five hours. That is all it took.

Was I *cured* then? Well, people often ask me that. They say, "What did she do to you?"

It is important to keep in mind that NLP is not a "Do To" process, it is a "Do With" process. It is a partnership, an exchange. It is a way of thinking too. Have you seen the Royal Marines' adverts? NLP is like that: it is A State Of Mind.

NLP all started in the early 70s when two guys called Richard Bandler (a maths student) and John Grinder (a linguistics professor), joined forces to study the excellent results that therapists Fritz Perls and Virginia Satir were achieving with their own individual clients.

Bandler and Grinder modelled what they were doing, broke it down into components, little bite-size chunks of excellence that they too could learn how to apply.

Then they focused on Milton Erickson, who was an American psychiatrist and psychologist specialising in medical hypnosis, and who was incredibly successful with his own clients – even though he was doing exactly the opposite of what Virginia Satir was doing.

Well, fancy that! So Bandler and Grinder modelled him, too.

All of this modelling stuff then gave birth to the Meta Model (based on Satir's approach), which is a linguistics tool that enables us to identify the deletions, distortions and generalisations in people's language.

For example, when I was depressed, I kept saying that I was drinking too much because the love of my life had left me. Not my fault, right? Poor little me, I was only the victim in all this. Well, an example of a good Meta Model question to challenge this very unhelpful thinking might be, "What specifically is it about this situation that makes you choose to drink?"

Boom! Putting the responsibility back on myself, putting me back in the only place where I can actually change my behaviour: by accepting responsibility for it.

The other famous NLP tool that came out of Bandler and Grinder's research was the Milton Model. Where Satir is specific, Erickson is not. He deals in the abstract. He uses hypnotic language.

An example of the Milton Model would be: "People can change and I know that you can, now, haven't you?" Using the uncharacteristic tag question at the end means that you have to agree with the statement that **you have changed already,** in order for the sentence to make sense. Maybe you will not agree by the way... well at least not consciously!

This is how hypnotic language is used in NLP: it is not mind-control for nefarious purposes as so many people have come to believe wrongly! In NLP we work with the unconscious mind, and this is how we do it. We do not try to bypass it, silence it or ignore it, instead we bring it on board.

Because let's face it, the unconscious mind is the one you really have to convince. In Coaching we often say that it is the "goal getter", whilst your conscious mind is only the "goal setter".

Say you decide you are going to be healthy from now on, you are feeling great about your decision, no more wine, no more pizza... And yet your unconscious mind might be standing in the background, arms folded, shaking her head, going, "Nope, I am not signing up for that!"

So be aware that whenever you are not getting the results that you want in your life, there is probably some kind of misalignment between your conscious and unconscious minds. Or a disconnection. NLP can help with that.

So, Grinder and Bandler eventually bundled their modelling techniques and own personal insights and learnings, and called the resulting method Neuro Linguistic

Programming. And in NLP we are very much aware that our mind, the language that we use to describe our experience, and our body, are all linked and in constant communication with each other.

If you think that the body is separate, think again…

Try this for example: make a ring with your index and ring fingers. Say what your name is out loud as you try to break the ring with your other index finger. My guess is you will not be able to. Now try again and this time say something that is completely not true for you. Like, I am an alien and I have three heads. My guess is that this time you will be able to easily break the ring. (At least I hope you will.)

Remember, we think we are our bodies, but really we are energy. How we shape that energy, with our thoughts, beliefs, values and language, determines not only our experience of the world we live in and how we perceive it, but also the shape and condition of our bodies.

For instance, I was out on a run last week when it started to rain like the world was about to end. And then it turned to hail, and it was incredibly windy too. I told myself, "I am freezing cold, and I absolutely hate this today!" Well guess what, all of a sudden the run turned a little bit harder! So I reverted back to my usual mantra: "I am strong and loose and running great" – and all of a sudden, it was much better and easier!

Language does matter, and so how can we use this to our

advantage?

Well, for starters we can start to pay attention to our words and choose them carefully, like my running example. What are you looking to achieve, what state of mind do you need to be in to be successful? Choose your internal dialogue wisely and use it for maximum positive effect:

Yes, You Can!

Also, I think it is nice to be a little creative with our words: the geek in me loves reading the Thesaurus! Words are great, so have many and love them all!

I know someone who has "a bit of a thing" against the US. Whatever it is, if it is American he makes an instant decision to dislike it. He hates the word "awesome", for example, and I really do feel a little bit sorry for him that he will never allow himself to ever feel "AWESOME!!"

Play with your words, too: don't just feel "good", feel "super-excellent" instead! Don't just "eat a meal", experience "a taste fiesta"! Use intense and vibrant words to describe each and every experience. Make your life come alive. Feel wicked-awesome about it!

A Recipe For Happiness

In NLP we know there are three things that can influence our behaviour:

1. The internal representations we hold inside our head
2. Our state (how we feel internally)
3. And our physiology

Ultimately our behaviour will influence our results, so it is a pretty important part of the entire process of being successful.

Let's have a closer look at it:

We know that our internal representations are the results of an event being run through a whole bunch of things we call our "filters" – things like our attitudes, values and beliefs, decisions and memories. These end up giving meaning to the event in question: bear in mind that it is not necessarily the right one, the true one, or the only one, since obviously everyone has different filters and therefore enjoys a different experience, but it is definitely the one for you.

This in turn pretty much informs your state:

Happy Internal Reps = Happy States = Open Relaxed Physiology = GREAT RESULTS!

An internal representation is the meaning that you give to an event. If there were no human beings on Earth, would there be any meaning to anything? Would it be bad or good that it is raining?

I was at work one morning a few years back, feeling awesome as it was! I had woken up really early, had a good run in the rain (which made all of the wonderful smells of early-morning countryside come alive.) Then I'd had a nice hot shower, a good breakfast, a happy drive to the office and a nice chat with one of my friends. Feeling great.

Then my colleague walked in, wet, grumpy, scowling, and she declared: "What a horrible, awful, miserable day today!"

By the way, how do you feel when you are reading this?

Exactly!

It was raining, and so she had decided that it was a horrible day. Now, of the two of us, which one do you think was going to have the best day? The best results? The best connections with other people?

So, when you assign a meaning to something, always make sure it is a positive one.

If something looks like a real challenge, maybe you have a leak through your roof as a result of all the rain, do it anyway. Of course it will be harder, but remember, if you assign a negative meaning to an event in your life, you will end up in a negative state, a negative physiology, and your results will suffer the same fate.

It is all about context, and this is how it works: one of the ways I learned to speak English was by reading books. At first, a lot of the times I simply took a stab at meaning based on the context around it. I kept it simple; if the story made sense overall I was happy, and it was only when I got older that the Thesaurus suddenly became interesting.

In NLP we know that all meaning is context dependent, and that is great because if you want to change the meaning of an event, you can do it simply by changing the context around it. What is context? My favourite thesaurus threw a nice chain of synonyms at me when I looked it up:

Context = Frame of Reference = Point of View = Attitude = **REACTION**.

So the meaning of a situation or event will simply depend on the way we choose to react to it.

For most people the idea that there is always a choice and that we are in charge is easy to adhere to, up to a certain point. In theory, we want to agree it is so. In practice, maybe it is a little harder. But the more you practice, the more you will see it reflected in your results positively.

And so when you are faced with an event in your life, if you feel strong negative emotions welling up inside of you, like anger, fear or panic, allow yourself a bit of breathing time to ask yourself: How can I assign a positive meaning to this situation? How can I make this event work for me?

Because there is always a way:

Your car got stolen? Won't you feel grateful for the opportunity to ride your bike more often when it helps you achieve your target weight quicker? You got bad reviews on a novel you wrote? How great that you got some feedback about what you can do better on your next one!

Some people are great at reframing and very good at finding all sorts of positives in their lives. Others... not so much. But you can always get better at it if that is what you want.

Here is the story of one of my clients, who successfully used NLP Coaching and techniques to help him through a period of redundancy at work.

- <u>Week One</u>:

The situation: being made redundant
The reaction: fear, panic, anxiety, depression
Outcome expectations: convinced he would not find another job, become unable to pay his bills, lose his house and end up on the street. (Sounded a little familiar to me

that one!)

To add insult to injury, all of a sudden it was as if all of the news media out there were doing stories on the economic crisis and on people who had been made homeless through redundancy. My client could not escape seeing it in the papers, hearing about it on the radio, he even started to meet people who were in that situation.

Now, this illustrates clearly what actually happens when you focus on something with enough intensity: you get more of it.

Time for a bit of anatomy: we all have something called the *Reticular Activating System,* located in the brain stem, which is responsible amongst other things for bringing relevant bits of information to our attention.

For example, have you ever decided to buy a new car, let's say a brand new Clio, and all of a sudden you start to see more of them on the roads, on TV and in magazines?

Thank your RAS for that. It has received instructions to focus on the car you want, and is actively picking them out for you.

This is important: whatever you choose to focus on, good or bad, you will start to experience more frequently in your life. That is how it works, no exceptions. The question is: how can you make the system work for you?

Here is how: ask yourself a lot of option-generating questions, focus on the solution, focus on what you want, and take appropriate action. See a coach to help you through it all if you need to.

Let's go back to our client now:

- <u>Week Two:</u>

The situation: being made redundant
The reaction: hope – a hint of excitement - looking at options!
Outcome expectations: client was powerfully in touch with his resources! Convinced he would be able to find another job within a week or so… maybe even a better job!

So what happened? Is it magic? Nope: simply NLP Coaching at its best.

No More Excuses!

I have mentioned a little earlier that we build our lives using what we call in NLP our Model of the World: a collection of personal beliefs and values, the basic structure behind our reality construct. None of it is real, but it is a tool we have at our disposal to experience life on Earth.

I know I sound like a broken record, but this is an important concept to understand.

And one of the first things we learn in NLP is that everyone's model of the world is different, and that it is important to respect how other people choose to shape their universe. It is also crucial to realise that we can all experience a different kind of life, just by changing our model of the world. Change how you think, change your world, it is as simple as that.

Another thing that is crucial to the notion of being able to achieve positive change in our lives is that it is a good thing to be at Cause for everything in it.

In NLP we call this The Cause and Effect equation, known as $C > E$. We call it an equation because it can only ever be one or the other. There is no such thing as being a little bit at Cause, or a little bit at Effect, depending on how you feel in the moment or what is happening to you.

Being at Cause means that we take one hundred percent responsibility for ourselves, our actions and our results.

I create my world, no one else does. So do you.

Now, I am not perfect (there is no such thing as perfection anyway, by the way) and so when I create greatness in my life, that is wonderful and I have no problem acknowledging that I am at Cause for it.

Taking responsibility for stuff that is not so good is more difficult… But it is not impossible, and here is a bit of an extreme example.

Again, a true personal story:

A few years ago I was driving back to Leicester from Norwich, where I had spent the day working with one of our sales guys. On the way home, a tractor with broken brakes came racing out of a side road, ploughed into my car and sent me flying into the path of an oncoming truck. The company car I was driving was a write-off with £8,000 worth of damage listed.

It turned out that the tractor had no brakes, so obviously it was not my fault. The police confirmed that, and the insurance company agreed as well, and awarded me a nice little settlement.

According to the rules of our modern society, I was definitely not responsible (at Cause) for what had happened. Not my fault, poor little me, I was the victim, that sort of thing. And a lot of people would be worried about me now if I started to say that I created that event...

But you know what, that is exactly right: I did create it.

At the time, I was experiencing a lot of negative emotions. This was in September 2008 and things were already not going great for me. Anger, sadness, hurt, fear and guilt were all competing for attention and arguing inside my head, and what was that like?

Well, let me tell you: it was utter chaos. What is a metaphor for chaos? A car crash. And it sounded like one too, with glass being smashed up, and metal getting bent out of shape; it was like dragging nails on a blackboard.

There is absolutely no doubt in my mind that I manifested that accident from all of the toxic stuff that was inside of me. It was that intense, that powerful. Now do you see what I mean about thoughts becoming reality?

Oh yes, for all of you out there who are fans of *The Secret,* this is the Law of Attraction in action right there.

So again, choose your thoughts *carefully*. And if you find yourself unable to choose happy thoughts, well I hope that you realise through reading my story that you can learn how to do it. Everybody can, and frankly I cannot understand why this sort of thing is not taught to us at school.

Also, I am not saying that taking a hundred percent responsibility for one's life is always going to be easy… Although you can make it as easy or as difficult as you want, of course.

What I am saying is that unless you are willing to look at your results and entertain the idea that you are responsible for them, all of them whatever they may be, completely, with zero exception, you will not be able to change anything.

Carl Jung, a Swiss psychiatrist and psychotherapist, and the founder of analytical psychology, said that "We cannot change anything until we accept it. Condemnation does not liberate, it oppresses."

This is probably one of my favourite quotes. So the next time you find yourself putting a lot of energy criticising something, disliking something, realise that all this negative energy you are putting into it is hurting you – no one else. If you do not like something, change it. If you do not want to change it, accept it, be totally cool with it.

This goes for anger too, and resentment especially. I used to hate my partner after we broke up, but the thing is, since we had no contact anymore who was I hurting by holding on to those feelings? Only me. So we all need to learn to forgive, really forgive ourselves and others, in order to be able to move on. We need to do it for ourselves.

Now, after reading my theory about that car accident some of you out there might be convinced that I have lost the plot, never regained it in fact, and wondering what on earth I am talking about and how all of this is even remotely connected to NLP.

Well, Coach and Master Trainer Adriana James recently wrote a great article on her website, nlpcoaching.com.

She said this: "[…] the materialist scientists will tell you that to believe that you can influence the future with your own mind, creativity and imagination and with the help of Time Line Therapy® is all a delusion. […]Then here is a question for you. We are deluded in many ways every single day of our lives believing in crap we're being served by the media. Why not believe in a "delusion" that produces some positive results?"

Why not indeed…

So, in NLP we believe that we are one hundred percent in charge of our mind, and one hundred percent in charge of our results.

Start to live your life in this way, and I guarantee that you will quickly realise this is far from a delusion.

Wishing Is Not Enough

Yes, I did watch *The Secret*, and yes, I did fall in love with the Law of Attraction.

But I did not automatically start to believe that it was some great big miracle that was going to make all of my dreams come true without any effort from me. Just sitting on the beach and thinking positive thoughts all day is not going to do it for you, folks!

I know that some people believe exactly that, and obviously always end up feeling disappointed and disillusioned. Then they quit. But the good news for them is that they have done some really good work already, are sending some great vibrations out there into the world and the universe, and so all they really need to do now is take some good old-fashioned elbow-grease type action!

Obviously, they have to be motivated to do that, and sometimes motivation can be lacking. The world is very sticky these days, don't you think? Life has become very busy, very difficult, very complicated.

And what is life all about, really?

I was asking myself that very same question a few years ago. It was late July, dark and raining, freezing cold, and I had been working late in the office on a project that meant absolutely nothing to me. I was going home to a tiny empty flat to cook myself a quick dinner and go to bed, just so that I could get up extra early the next day and do it all over again.

How depressing.

And the question I was asking myself was not "why" do I keep doing it; after all I knew why… I had bills to pay and I needed to eat and keep a roof over my head, like we all do. What I was asking myself was "how" can I do it differently?

How could I put pleasure, excitement and joy back into my life?

It seems to me this is a question many people struggle to find an answer to. A lot of people do not even bother to ask anymore. This is how tired, weary and resigned we have become.

How many times have you heard people say, "Well, I am not so happy in my job right now, but I don't know what else I could be doing. If I knew what I want to do I would go and do it, but…I just don't know what, how, who I want to be."

Maybe this is the sort of thing you even say to yourself sometimes?

And so you go home after work, have a drink and watch mindless TV to try to forget about things for a while (and who can blame you really), and so it goes. Before you know it, another week goes by, another month, another year, and there you are, still stuck in the same meaningless life, believing that is all there is and all that you can do.

I used to look at my life often and think, "If only I could buy a house", "If only I could play the guitar", "If only I could lose some weight"… then I would be happy.

Little did I know that I was going at it all wrong! Because you have to **be** happy first, then you can **have** the things you dream of. Having things only comes as a direct result of who you are being.

Of course, being happy "right now" is not hard, all you need to do is think of happy stuff. There, you happy? Yes, there is much more to it than that. But you do need to feel good in life, about your life, and yourself in general, because you will never be able to build anything that you truly desire on a foundation of feeling bad, sad, depressed, angry of resentful.

Now, maybe being happy, long term contentment, also means living a meaningful and authentic life. Just being true to yourself and who you are, correct? Who thinks that this is not something you can achieve? My guess would be quite a lot of people.

In NLP everything we do is designed to increase wholeness. The dictionary definition of "whole" is as follows: "In an unbroken and undamaged state; in one piece."

A lot of people will have seen the news headlines about Frank Maloney, boxing manager and former promoter of heavyweight World Champion Lennox Lewis, who at the age of sixty-one underwent gender reassignment. After years of struggle and a suicide attempt, Kellie has claimed her decision to reveal she is now living as a woman felt like "a complete release." She said, "I can do anything now, because I am not living two lives anymore."

Wow… Imagine spending sixty-one years in someone else's skin…

Being whole, being congruent, and being true to who you are: it is important.

So how can you find your true passion in life? How can you discover who you are really meant to be, when you are spending your days working for somebody else, with barely a minute to think your own thoughts?

Here is how to kick-start your life and bring the fun and joy back into it:

- **Step 1: ask yourself a simple question.**

If you suddenly found out that the world was going to end tomorrow, what would your number one regret be? Write it down.

"My number one regret would be _____."

- **Step 2: ask yourself another question.**

"What stops me doing _____(insert regret)_____ right now?"
Have a little brainstorm with yourself, write it all down, and then pick the top three.

- **Step 3: keep asking questions!**

This time you want to look at your top three and ask yourself, "Is this really true"?

For example, if the world ended tomorrow, my biggest regret would have been that I had never got to be a writer.

Being a writer was my dream. When I was eleven years old I even created a little newspaper with my sister. We would write poems and stories about our town and our friends and family, and then give it to my dad to type it all up and sell it to people. Good business minds already!

But then for many years I stopped writing, although my dream never really went away. And like I said before, if I want to be a writer, all I need to do is write, right? What was I waiting for? What was stopping me? Well, my top three reasons were:

    1 – I have nothing to talk about
    2 – It will not be good enough to publish
    3 – I am just not good enough (that one again, rearing

its ugly head!)

When I went through Step 3., when I started to question those beliefs and put them to the test, to my astonishment, I realised that none of my reasons stood up to scrutiny. And you know what, I got a little bit excited then. And I got busy with some good old-fashioned elbow-grease type action! I started to live on purpose.

Is Ignorance Really Bliss?

Do you do affirmations?

I read Louise Hay a few years ago and I thought great, I will do affirmations from now on! And I will do the Jack Canfield trick of sticking a cheque for £100,000 on the ceiling above my bed, and then done! I will get what I want. Problem is, I am short sighted, so when I woke up the cheque was just a blur and too far for me to see (what a great metaphor for how I thought about my goal!), and also when I did affirmations, the little voice inside of me was having a laugh - it giggled, "Hey, nice try, blah blah blah, but you know that's not true, right?"

I realised that the little voice had a point. It was not true, I did not really believe that I could. I used to look at the people out there who achieved their dreams and lived the life they really wanted, by design, and I used to think that was great, but something in me also believed that they were different.

"People like them", could realise their dreams. People like me, well, we could not. People like me just read the self-help books, created the vision boards, said all the affirmations, but we did not really believe that we could change anything. I did not know how to bridge the gap, how to jump over to join the people who could. Did I actually think that I could be like them? Not really. Deep down I did not believe that stuff like that happened to people like me… and this last sentence was definitely part of the problem!

Now I phrase it a little differently, because I know that people like me can make stuff like that happen. And I have and continue to do so, and thinking differently with NLP was the starting point of every success I have had since. I also have some tips on how you can make this happen for yourself, which I will share with you in the last part of this book.

So then, as you may have guessed from our earlier exercise, we ask a lot of questions in NLP Coaching. Just keep in mind that those beliefs you have about yourself, about what you can or cannot do, are just beliefs: they are only true if you decide to make them true, and if they do not serve you, elevate and empower you to achieve your goals, then you can change them, as and when you decide to.

As a coach, my job is to help you with a few really essential things – not to do them for you, or tell you what to do, but to facilitate the process.

My aim is to help you identify your goals, both short and long term; identify what stops you achieving them (or even just starting!); letting go of any limiting beliefs you may have lurking inside your head, those like "I am not good enough", or "things like that do not happen to people like me"; and then we can put a bullet-proof plan of action in place, and allow you to work through it, step by step. As we say in running: nice and steady.

Remember, there are not many things that you cannot achieve, if you really put your mind to it. If you clear your stuff and focus on what you want, you cannot not achieve your dreams. So my question to you is: **what are you going to do now?** Because it is up to you.

One of my friends phoned me up the other day, and she was absolutely fuming.

She had had a really bad day at work. Her car had broken down on the way home. Now she had just realised that she had forgotten the one little thing that she had walked all the way to the shops to buy, and so could not cook the meal she had been looking forward to all day.

Basically you could say she was a little bit fed up with everything!

"Sometimes I wish I did not know that cheesecake and alcohol are bad for me," she declared over the phone, boiling. "Sometimes I wish I had never heard of the power of raw kale, interval training, meditation and Jack Canfield. I want chips drowned in cheese and mayonnaise! I want the biggest TV I can get my hands on! I want a subscription to OK! Magazine so I can read about other people's cellulite issues and feel good about myself! I want to unplug my brain and embrace my inner physical and spiritual slob."

And… wait a minute.

> "Do you really?" I asked.
> "Yes," she said, "because ignorance is bliss!"

Wow. What a statement. When people say that do they really believe it is true?

Or do they mean in fact that ignorance is easy? Because I guess if you did not know you could improve you would not have to try, right? If you did not know that people are lying to you, you would not have to search for the truth, would you? Sometimes knowing things… it can make you feel a little uncomfortable.

But if you did not know, would you not also be unaware of not knowing, and would it not prevent you from experiencing the very "easiness" that you seek? How much ignorance is required before you feel good? How much of a coma do you have to be in before you start to be happy?

When people say ignorance is bliss do they mean in fact that life is hard? And if it is, who makes it hard? Is it hard all the time? And maybe there is good hard, like when you make it to the top of a tough climb on your bike, and bad hard, like when you lose someone you love.

So then, when it is bad, how can you make it good?

Questions, questions… When you think about the magnitude of everything that you do not know does it make your head spin? It certainly does mine!

But I think the best part about ignorance is becoming aware of it, bringing it into the light. Because then you can choose. Will you decide to really light it up and learn as much as you can? Or will you ignore it and carry on as you were? Some people do. Choosing to live your life wide awake is not for everyone. Because once you become aware, there is no way back to the way it was before either.

Once you take that little red pill, that is it, you are changed forever. Eyes wide open, it is a very different sort of world, you know. And once you get a glimpse of what is waiting for you on the other side of the hard and the difficult, you are going to want a piece of it.

An old work colleague once told me that she could not drive on the motorway. I said, "Great! Do you want to change that belief?" She looked horrified. She said, "Oh no, I can't change. I don't do motorways. Never have. I simply can't do it."

Now, I was born in France, grew up there, and learned to drive on the right side of the road. Then I moved to England and simply switched sides. I can drive on the motorway, no problem! So if a French girl who learned to drive on the wrong side of the road can do it, why can't my colleague?

Isn't it funny what we choose to believe?

Ignorance is bliss… When people say that do they mean in

fact that it is safe?

Because with knowledge comes empowerment, responsibility, and risk taking. You do not let yourself off the hook anymore. You have to find the scariest thing there is out there for you, and go do it. You feel compelled. You have a duty now to live up to your full potential. It is like this beating drum inside your heart that keeps saying, "Now you can, Now you can, Now you can… Get up and do it!"

The consequence of trying might be that one day you succeed… Just ask Bradley Wiggins if it was not worth it!

And there is something else as well. You know the fun bit about choice?

It is that sometimes you can choose to give yourself a break too. Sometimes you can have those chips and cover them up in delicious, extra-strong, mature cheddar, and dissolve in that bliss! The next day you are up at five and in the gym, sipping your kale and ginger smoothie, dripping sweat onto your copy of the Success Principles. Smiling.

Because I have said that NLP is about increasing wholeness, and it is also about increasing choice.

The term we use in Coaching when we work with you is "change work" – well yes, once we are done you will achieve the change that you want, you will be thinking differently, and your problem will be gone. But we will not take the unwanted behaviours away; we will simply give you some new, positive and empowering ones. Then it is up to you.

You know, I could do self-harming again if I wanted to. I could do depressed as well, although because of how much I have changed, it would be much harder for me now. And the fact is that I can do the opposite of these two things because I have options, I have awareness, and I have choices.

One thing us coaches often say to our clients is that You Have To Focus On What You Want.

NLP is not some magic wand that I am going to wave over your head to make everything better. Change requires intensity, desire, absolute total dedication. You have to work at it. But trust me, it does get easier, and that is the whole point of having resources and knowing how to think a little differently.

Now that, my friends, is bliss.

There Is No Truth

So what do you believe, and how do you know that those beliefs are true? Because you got them from your parents? From your teachers? From your church? Oh, hang on, maybe it was from the BBC, right?

I have just read another one of Adriana James' articles on nlpcoaching.com, entitled *"What Has "Interstellar" to do with NLP Thinking"*.

In it, Adriana makes a very interesting comment about the film and specifically her thinking strategy as she was watching it:

> "[…] the movie was very informative (if you can watch it with a trained mind, and that's not a small task). It was also a very interesting movie especially when – with an NLP trained mind – you're able to observe the social memes [...] And what a better way of inserting memes into the culture of a society than movies. Most people watch movies for entertainment not for information […]"

Some people out there are probably still convinced that NLP is all about mind control and woe betide anyone who looks me in the eye… What they do not realise is that NLP techniques are about the very thing they desire:

freedom of mind, and freedom of thought.

Being able to "think NLP" enables us to discover a new layer of information in almost everything, whether it is a movie, a situation at work, watching the news or reading an article in the paper.

That is empowerment, folks.

What is it? What is it not? What else could it be? What is the purpose for it? By asking the right questions we can expand our perception. We can see the big picture instead of getting lost in the details. We can connect the dots.

When we think NLP we become able to choose our beliefs, not use other people's. Not ready-made ones. We can start to make intelligent decisions about our lives according to what our critical mind has to say about it.

Because let's take nutrition for example. What a minefield!

Should I go full-on vegan like ultra-marathon legend Scott Jurek? Have Pizza Hut deliver to me during my long runs like Dean Karnazes, who is also an ultra-marathon runner? Or should I just do a hundred percent Paleo like Christmas Abbott, the Crossfit champion?

I have tried so many things that sounded great but did not work, not just about nutrition obviously, and the great thing about that is that now I know what the secret is.

The truth simply is not out there. Sorry, Mulder!

Here is a great story taken from *The Magic of Metaphor: 77 Stories for Teachers, Trainers and Thinkers* by Nick Owen:

"There is an ancient tale that says it was not long after the Gods had created humankind that they began to realise their mistake.

The creature they had created were so adept, so skillful, so full of curiosity and the spirit of enquiry that it was only a matter of time before they would start to challenge the Gods themselves for supremacy.

All the Gods were very clear about one thing. The difference between them and mortals was the difference between the quality of the resources they had. While humans had their egos and were concerned with the external, material aspects of the world, the Gods had spirit, soul, and an understanding of the workings of the inner self.

The danger was that sooner or later the humans would want some of that too. So the Gods decided to hide their precious resources. And after much searching and debating, one God came up with the ultimate secret place.

"Why don't we hide these resources inside each human?" he suggested. "They'll never think to look for them there..."

So what if the truth we seek was in each and every one of us? What if people had all the resources they need to succeed and to achieve their desired outcomes, deep down inside? What then?

Tell me, what do you believe about yourself?

You can't sing, you can't run, you're too fat, too tall, too French, too dumb, not good enough, afraid of public speaking and scared of heights. There. Enough labels for you?

Why don't you take them all off and have a good look at them?

For example, okay, so you are afraid of public speaking. Did you know that this is actually the number one phobia in America? Twenty-five percent of all Americans are terrified of public speaking, even more afraid of that than death! Well, I used to be terrified of it. If given a choice of doing public speaking or jumping out of a plane without a parachute, I would have said Hey, no problem, just get me on that plane!

But what would it feel like to be a confident, really good public speaker? What would it take to be able to really enjoy myself when I was up there on that stage? I really wanted to find out. I thought I had it in me to become a really good presenter. And so using our NLP Belief Change technique is how I got rid of my fear of public speaking, on Day Four of my very first training.

Understand this: if you know something, then you also know its opposite. You can tell something is red because you know what red is not; you know when it is dark because you know when there is light; and so if you think you are not good enough, it also means that you know what good enough looks like.

Shift your thinking.

In NLP we say that there are no unresourceful people, only unresourceful states. And if you can imagine yourself doing something, that means you have the resources inside of you to be successful at it, otherwise you would not be able to even start to think about it.

Makes sense?

Napoleon Hill, author and advisor to President F.D Roosevelt, famously said "What the mind of man can conceive and believe, it can achieve." Now, the Internet is awash with feel-good motivational quotes like this and it is "nice" to read them, but I think most people do not realise that there is also a deeper truth to them, another layer. I know I used to.

The thing is, when you begin to understand the science behind the words, once you understand how the mind really works and what it can do for you, everything changes. Because the stuff you thought was just feel-good quotes on the Internet becomes real possibility.

And the truth really is nothing more than what you want to make it. The truth is what works for you. You can build your own world from the inside out if you decide to, simply by choosing your beliefs.

You will know which beliefs are right for you because they will resonate within. They will shine brighter than anything else around. They will simply feel good, and that is when you will know you have found your truth. And it does not matter what it is or how crazy it seems to other people, so long as it makes your heart beat faster.

With NLP you can turn your fears into excitement.

Huge claim, right? Outrageous, yes? Surely this is just manipulative rubbish? Well, not when you can make it happen. I have, and that means you can too.

There is no truth. Scary or Exciting?

You decide.

SWITCH ON!

PART THREE: TOP TIPS FOR LIVING

Help And Where To Get It

Now this is going to be a really enjoyable part of the book for me to write, because this is where I get to share all the little day to day things that work for me in order to "keep my bin clean", as my NLP coach Julie used to say.

Keeping your bin clean means that you stay the course on whatever your goals are: for me the main one at the time was to make sure that I did not fall back into a destructive thinking pattern again. These days the techniques I will share with you have simply become a way of life for me. I always have something going on, a goal or a project. I feel excited. I keep myself busy because I want to keep on growing, keep on creating a life that I enjoy. And the minute you get comfortable, you stop growing. So I keep moving, I keep challenging myself, I keep learning. Like I said before, it is a state of mind.

Before I start to give you tips though, I would like to give you a little bit more info on where and how you can get the help you need, should you need it and want it, and as always, it is based on what worked for me.

What I would say to you is that, if you know what it is like to feel a little bit stuck in life, if you have this sense that there is something more out there, just that little bit out of your reach, then you are reading the right book, and you have come to the right place. This is not a coincidence!

Congratulations, too, because if you are reading this it means that you are looking for solutions, and that you are already bringing empowerment into your life, and taking action on the things you want.

So, well done!

As we have discussed before, maybe you have beliefs that you are "not good enough", "can't make enough money", or "don't deserve a great job". Or maybe you want to lose weight or stop smoking. Perhaps, like I used to, you are struggling with depression and/or self-harming. Maybe you just want to "figure things out", or perhaps you are really far advanced and you already have a bunch of goals you want to work on and realise.

The first thing to remember is that if you are seeing a doctor, doing therapy already, anything like that, this is good and you do not need to stop. You can do NLP on the side. If you are taking anti-depressants and want to stop, check with your doctor first.

If you are looking to do NLP with someone, find yourself a coach or master practitioner who is ABNLP trained.

ABNLP stands for the American Board of NLP, and this is what they want you to know about the services that we offer:

"Remember that NLP is complementary healthcare. The self-regulated holistic treatments and client-centered disciplines in which NLP coaches are trained and experienced in include:

- Consulting and coaching,
- Time Line Therapy™ techniques,
- Neuro Linguistic Programming and
- Hypnosis.

Your coach should always provide only those services in which they have been trained, and if they find that they cannot help you, they will refer you to a licensed professional who can.

Throughout the world, the standards for each of the membership levels are extremely high, and so I would always recommend working with ABNLP Approved Coaches. Every time you see the seal of the ABNLP on a practitioner's website, you can rest assured that a high level of excellence will be available to you throughout your coaching relationship."

If you do not see a seal, then make sure you find out what your coach's qualifications are, and check them out for yourself. There are a lot of brilliant people out there doing Life Coaching and a whole bunch of different things, and some of them are excellent. I am ABNLP trained, and the coach I worked with to overcome severe clinical depression and self-harming tendencies was also ABNLP trained. And this is all I have to say on the subject!

Of course you might also wonder what would be the benefit to you of hiring a coach, instead of the do-it-yourself approach. Well, I have experienced both, so let me tell you a little bit about that.

Self-help books, tapes and videos are wonderful because they can provide huge motivation for change; if you get a good book, like Tony Robbins' *Awaken The Giant Within* for example, you will be in extremely good hands. If you do all the exercises in the book, great. If you stick with the coaching programme, even better! The thing with books though is that it is easy to put them down and lose sight of them once you have read them once. You may feel incredibly inspired one minute, and completely forget about it the next.

You see, you might get a great idea for a project or discover something new that really appeals to you, and when you do you will get excited and motivated straight away. All good so far. So you go to work feeling wonderful that day, you might even tell your colleagues about it, but by the time you get home, tired, hungry, and having had time to settle a bit, perhaps you are not as motivated as you were initially. Sound familiar?

Allow yourself to watch a little bit of TV and sleep on it, and chances are that this thing that really got you buzzing, whether it was taking a training, applying for a new job, losing weight or sky-diving for charity, will never see the light of day.

If you hire a coach on the other hand, as part of your coaching agreement with them, one of their jobs will be to keep you on track, and completely accountable throughout the process; not accountable to them, obviously, but to yourself. They will support you when the going gets tough, and they will never let you quit.

With efficient tasking and strategies, through a high-level partnership which is designed with yourself in order to bring the best out of you, they will help to keep your passion, excitement and motivation alive and burning bright, all the way to the finish line…

And way, way beyond!

Oh, whilst I am on the subject, another quick thing to mention before I move on to tips and techniques that work: one of the things that your coach will help you with as well is define an evidence procedure for your goals.

Meaning that you will write down in black and white what it will look like once your goal has been achieved. You will identify the very last thing that needs to happen for you to know you have achieved your goal. You might find this amusing, but I once decided on a goal, worked at it, achieved it, and never even knew it! Believe me, it is easily done, although of course when I did that I was not NLP qualified yet! Okay.

Keep Your Bin Clean

A lot of people ask me if the change will be instant. The answer is both yes… and no!

What will be instant is the realisation that you never had a problem in the first place, and then you will change immediately. But in this reality of flesh, blood, and solid brick buildings, in order for that change to become long-lasting and permanent, you are going to have to work at it a little.

This means focusing on what you want, and doing what you need to do to cement that change within yourself. Remember it takes around twenty-one days to form a new habit, so whatever you are doing, keep doing it! And part of how you do this is by keeping your bin clean, as I mentioned before.

I am going to share with you some specific tips, a few precious little things that I do, some techniques that I use, a way of thinking that absolutely guarantee that I stay on track with my goals and the vision I have defined for myself. Here it is right there: "To live an authentic life and to be true to myself in every aspect of it; therefore creating success, happiness and joy, and inspiring the people around me to be all that they can be: EVERY – SINGLE – DAY."

What vision do you have for yourself? What is your mission, what is your life statement? If you think that you were born by accident, think again! We are all here for a very specific reason, we all have something to offer and contribute to this wonderful puzzle that is the world. We are all individual pieces of it, and it would not be complete without you. So be happy that you are here and find your purpose.

Remember, we are all part of something much bigger than we sometimes realise, and we need to allow ourselves to play the part that we were created for.

Our life's purpose is simply this: to be ourselves. To find that little spark of uniqueness and passion that we are on this planet to express, to create, to share with other people.

Think about what your life is all about and write it down in the space below:

TOP TIP # 1: BE AT CAUSE FOR EVERYTHING

Ever noticed how sometimes the only way to join in with the conversations in the office is to engage in collective moaning about, oh, let's say, your boss or your colleague?

Do you do it? Do you get angry or sad because other people make you feel a certain way? Do you blame it all on the traffic, the government, your boss, your co-workers, or your mother? (Your mother is always a good one, right?)

Well, I have good news for you guys, because now you can stop doing that.

Remember my earlier example that I was drinking too much because my partner had left me? What a cop-out that was, right? Can you see that?

Who went to the shop to buy the wine? Me.
Who chose to drink the whole bottle? Me.
Who chose to be hungover the next day? Me.

Always, always, me. But my default setting at the time was to be a victim. And I was using excuses in my work as well. I would say things like, "I can't go on this business trip because I am depressed, it will be too much for me and I will not be able to cope." Or, "I know I am not making any efforts to get on with my colleagues, but I suffer from depression after all, so people should just be nice to me instead."

Excuses, excuses…

Now, as long as you push the cause of feeling or acting a certain way onto something or someone else, do you realise what you make happen?

You give your power away.

You can only ever change something when you accept that you are doing it, that you are creating it. If you give other people your personal power, guess what, they will not be using it to make you feel good!

So the next time you are engaging in the blame game, (and I am not saying it does not feel good sometimes to have a good moan with your friends), but be realistic about it at least. Know that you are responsible for your results.

If you do not like the ones that you are getting, that is okay. You can get better results by changing the way you go about it. Remember, there is no failure, only feedback! Just do not let go of the power to do something about what is not going well in your life, by simply blaming somebody else for it.

Also, the next time you want to slag someone off, count to ten and do something else. If you say negative things about someone else, your unconscious mind will take it personally. Yes, that is right, your unconscious mind takes everything personally and relates it back to you. So when you say bad things about someone behind their back, it all falls back on you.

You have the choice between churning up a lot of negative energy with the words you use and the things you choose to say, and as a result get more negative energy pouring into your life. Or you can do the opposite and create good strong positive energy. Remember that you get what you focus on. Energy flows where attention goes. So I know which one I would choose.

Also, there is this thing in NLP that we call Perception is Projection. It is based on the idea that you only ever see on the outside what is already inside your mind. The world outside is pretty much a mirror of what is in your head.

So if your boss is doing your head in because he is so patronizing, then take a second or two to think about it, and ask yourself if maybe a part of you is not exactly the same. If your colleague is always rude to you, then again, have a little think about that.

It was a tough one to get my head around, but it is true that we often see things in other people that we need to resolve in ourselves. By becoming aware of those things which are still an issue within us, we can deal with them and grow as human beings. Try it for yourself: after a while it does become fun, I promise.

In NLP we talk about the "Law of Requisite Variety", which basically means that in any given system that part of the system with the most flexibility will control it. For us, this means that flexibility of behaviour is key; you have to be able to be flexible enough to produce the behaviour that is going to create the best results.

Quite often this is likened to looking into a mirror. If you do not like your hair when you look in the mirror, you just change your hair, right? You do not ask the mirror to show you something else. Life really does work like this, even though it seems weird and crazy and like a lot of hard work at first. You get out what you put in. If you do not like the things on the outside you have to change yourself on the inside first. Basically you just have to change your mind.

Last but not least: if you have constructive feedback for someone, make sure that they are happy to receive it first. And be gentle with it too. If someone does not truly want to change, you cannot force the change on them. And everybody has to follow their own path, experience their own journey, in their own time…

★

TOP TIP # 2: BE THE CHANGE YOU WANT TO SEE…

This is actually a quote from Mahatma Gandhi, "Be the change that you wish to see in the world." Here is a cool little story about Ghandi:

One day this woman came to see him, with her young son in tow, and she asked him, "Please would you tell my son to stop eating sugar? It is not good for his health." Ghandi glanced at the little boy and smiled. "Come back and see me in three weeks," he told the woman.

She went away, a little bit puzzled, and came back again three weeks later. "Please would you tell my son to stop eating sugar?" she asked again. "It is not good for his health."

And Ghandi did tell the little boy exactly that. This coming from such a powerful man had a huge effect on the little boy, who promised that he would be careful with sugar from now on. The mother was very happy, she thanked Ghandi profusely, and then she asked: "By the way, why did you ask me to come back, three weeks ago? I don't understand."

Ghandi smiled at her and nodded: "Three weeks

ago," he told her gently, "I myself was eating sugar."

This is a great little metaphor, don't you think? If you are fed up with certain behaviours in people, whatever those behaviours may be, then make sure that you do not perpetuate them, and that you do the exact opposite.

For example, how many times did I hear people in the office where I used to work complain that their colleagues were "miserable"? That they barely said hello, that they were always in a bad mood, etc., etc. I used to do it. Yet when I looked at the person making that comment, they were exactly the same! They complained, they were always in a bad mood, they never said hello… Again, I am speaking from personal experience here, because I used to be that person before I decided to change.

What about you? Do you say hi to everyone in the office? Are you a polite driver? Do you smile at the person behind the check-out in the supermarket? If not, then start doing it. It is amazing how incredible you can feel just by making one other person smile. Have a little chat, get some humanity going. It will make you feel fantastic.

Think of Louis Armstrong's famous song:

When you're smilin' keep on smilin'
The whole world smiles with you
And when you're laughin' oh when you're laughin'
The sun comes shinin' through

Spread a little joy. Be the change you want to see. It is not your job, how much money you make or how many cars you have that people will remember about you, it is how you make them feel.

So be loving! Be compassionate! Shine! Really make an effort to see the person behind the job, behind the title, behind the annoying behaviour that they do.

All of us on this planet so often fall for the idea that we are separate from one another, when in fact this could not be further from the truth. It is as if a bunch of waves suddenly started to think that they are separate, when in fact they are simply the ocean.

One of the most important and significant principles of quantum physics is referred to as Quantum Entanglement. It is defined when multiple particles are all linked together in such a way, that when you measure one of them, that particular measurement will influence the possible state of the other particles. See? We think they are separate, to all intents and purposes they are, but they are still connected – they are still one, as are we.

So when we take care of each other, really we are taking care of ourselves. Believe me, this is the hardest lesson for me to put into practice!

Because not everybody thinks that way, and sometimes it can feel like a very long one-way street. When you open your heart to people most of the times they will respond in kind. But a minority will take that as an open invitation to be rude, and walk all over you.

In NLP we say people always do the best they can with the resources they have available. We also believe that "people are not their behaviours", and that we should "accept the person, and change the behaviour." Not "excuse" the behaviour, not "allow" it, but change it.

Sometimes by being the change you want to see you will bring about the same change in other people. Sometimes, no matter what you do and how much you try, people will still remain shut-down and persist in their unwanted ways.

Well that is fine. They are simply not ready yet.

And what it means is that it is also okay for you to move on, and surround yourself with the ones who have learned to live from the heart. To live in love, and not in fear. And don't worry: sooner or later, everybody else will catch up.

★

TOP TIP # 3: DO IT FOR YOURSELF

What do you really want? What are you shooting for? Who do you want to please with your choices, the goals you have in life, and the actions you take to achieve them?

Because it should only be yourself, you know. And no, absolutely not, it is not selfish. It is just natural, it is what life is all about. In NLP we believe and insist that every goal should always be self-initiated and self-maintained.

How we ensure that what we do is "right" is by putting the emphasis on ecology. What is ecology? It is is the study of consequences. As a coach, whenever I do change work with a client, I always check that the consequences for everyone involved are positive: not only for my client, but also for their friends, family, work, society in general, and the planet as a whole. If something is not totally ecological then we do something else, simple as that.

So, lose weight because you want to be healthy, not because you want your partner to like you better; if you train for a marathon, do it because it makes you feel good, not because you want to impress anyone.

I know people who always make choices based on what other people want. Their spouse, their children, their friends, their boss. Some even choose careers they hate simply because of what their family have decided they want them to do.

Other people always make their choices based on what they "assume" other people will be happy with. They sacrifice themselves when no one even asked them to, and they blame it on other people when their life does not turn out exactly the way they had always wanted. And tell you what, most of the times they are wrong in their assumption of what these other people really wanted them to do… or that they even cared in the first place.

So take a moment to think about what you really want to achieve in your life. Make a list of all the things that you want to do, the sort of person you want to be, the things you want to have.

Get in touch with your unconscious mind and that little voice in your head that might tell you, "Hey, you always wanted to be an artist when you were little…"

Here is a true life story: when my sister was a little girl she started to develop a very big passion for everything connected to Canada.

And that was a bit strange, because we had no family over there, and my sister and I both grew up in the South of France. The weather for one is incredibly different as you can imagine. I always loved those long hot summers, but my sister for some reason was in love with snow. The walls of her bedroom were covered with pictures of

Canadian forests in the winter. She had pictures of Montreal on the walls. She even wanted my parents to buy her a husky!

She kept saying that when she grew up she would go live in Canada – and everyone around her would tell her that it was an impossible dream and to just forget about it: "You will do what everybody else does," they said, "you will stay here, get married, have kids, and that'll be it." Just like everyone else…

Well, a few years ago, I was already living in the UK by then, and my sister put a photo on Facebook that really got my attention. I do not particularly like Facebook by the way, but it is a good way to keep in touch with everyone, since I live in England, my parents are in France, my aunt in Florida, and guess what, yes indeed, my sister lives in Montreal!

The photo she put online was of herself standing on a rock on the side of a lake, and I had seen that rock before you know, I had seen that lake before. It was a photo she used to have on her bedroom wall, when she was a little girl and dreaming of going to live in Canada… And all the people who had told her when she was growing up that she would never be able to live her dream are still talking about it!

So whatever you do, make sure that you live your true passion in life, be true to who you are, and go for it!

★

TOP TIP # 4: CHOOSE TO THINK DIFFERENTLY

Right, now this is my favourite one! Whenever people ask me how I managed to recover from depression, I always mention NLP, and also that: "I chose to start thinking differently."

My life did not change, *I* changed it.

So I really want to share that with you now, because it is clear to me that many out there still believe they are at the mercy of their emotions; that they cannot be in charge of their mind; and that their results are way out of their control – Listen: it does not have to be this way!

I am going to quote from an article I read recently on the Huffington Post website, about living with anxiety and how to cope with it. I am excited about that article. Not because of the content, but because of the way it was written. The words it uses and the assumptions it contains make for an excellent case study.

"Anxiety is not something that I can control or just change whenever I want to. If I could just choose not to be anxious, I would. Since I can't, I've had to find ways to cope with it. Having anxiety is one of the most annoying things to live with

day to day."

So if you met someone for the first time, say at a party, and they told you this stuff, how would you feel? How would you react? Not a lot you can say in response, right? Just kind of depressing really.

I'll tell you what I would have done in the old days, before my NLP training: smiled politely (or not for that matter!) and moved on as quickly as I could!

Now let's imagine you are a trained coach of NLP – now when your client walks in and dumps this on your lap, you will be smiling. Obviously, maybe do not do it openly: one of the first rules of Rapport is, do not laugh at your clients!

Do allow yourself to be quietly excited though, because when a client comes to you with this sort of statement, it is like a gift. As a coach, you will have the perfect tools to do much better than simply cringe and run away: you will be able to contribute something really meaningful to the way your client sees their situation.

Let me show you how, by picking this little quote apart:

- *"Anxiety is not something that I can control or just change whenever I want to."*

What I would do with this sentence is change it to:

"Anxiety is not something that I have been able to

control in the past, yet."

- *"If I could just choose not to be anxious, I would."*

This I would change to:

"When I learn how to create a state of calm and serenity, then I definitely will be able to choose that."

In the first two sentences the person is on the Effect side of things. Not at cause, not responsible. She has decided and is affirming to herself that she is powerless to do something else. In my example we bring possibility back into it. Also, we turn the sentence into a positive. Your unconscious mind does not deal in negatives, you see.

If you say to yourself, "don't be anxious", the only thing your unconscious mind will hear is the word "anxious". So use positive language in everything. Mother Teresa famously always refused to go to anti-war rallies. She would say, "if you have a pro-peace one then I will come."

Makes sense?

Okay, let's carry on:

- *"Since I can't, I've had to find ways to cope with it."*

In this one, again, she is affirming that she "can't", and so she has "had to" find ways to cope with it.

"Had to"? Tell you what, if you do things in life because

you have to then you are definitely missing the point. Also, what is this coping business all about? Is that all that people aspire to these days, to cope and make-do?

Guys, we can do much better than that: we can thrive!!

- *"Having anxiety is one of the most annoying things to live with day to day."*

Again, this is such a disempowering way to look at it. Anxiety is not something you "have", it is something that you "do". So is depression, by the way. Everything is a behaviour at its core. Everything has a strategy.

I know, I know, we are not used to thinking in this way…

That is why this Top Tip is called "Think Differently"!

Listen, you can choose to believe this is all rubbish, or you can choose to believe this stuff works. Now, what would the difference be?

It is not about right or wrong, true or false, it is simply about what you decide to believe. What value would there be in believing that you cannot?

A colleague of mine recently said of hypnotherapy, "but you would have to believe in this stuff for it to work, right?" Well, if you had a problem and someone offered you a solution, why on earth would you want to declare it will not be useful to you? Would it not be better to have an open mind, to start believing that change is possible, that you can achieve the results you really want?

Might as well believe something that empowers you, right?

And again, this little shift in thinking might not happen instantly, for some people it takes a little practice. But results will come to you quickly once you have mastered it, and if you start to think in possibilities.

I changed my thinking, and it saved my life, so…

★

TOP TIP # 5: ACT "AS IF NOW"

In NLP we do not just have goals, we have SMART goals. Now obviously NLP did not invent this, and you have probably heard of it before, maybe at work; but some of the NLP words that go with the letters might be new to you. I mention it anyway because it is important. Goals have to be SMART.

- **S:** Specific, Simple
- **M:** Measurable, Meaningful to you
- **A:** <u>As if now</u>, Achievable, All areas of your life
- **R:** Realistic, Responsible / Ecological
- **T:** Timed, Toward what you want

Successful people use smart goals.

Another thing that they do and which has been absolutely essential in my own success is that they simply turn themselves into the person they want to be.

They act **"As If Now."**

When I started to apply this concept to my own life things started to change for me, and fast! Was it a bit funny sometimes calling myself something that I was not, yet, or doing "pretend" stuff? Yes. But I chose to ignore that and

I kept on doing it until I started to grow into it.

Successful people consistently act like the person they want to become; they adopt an attitude and create events in their lives that will be routine once they are that person. They do not simply sit there and wait for it to happen, they make it happen.

And then once they get the results, it is as if the results are actually just catching up with them. Understand this: first you have to become the person you want to be, then, and only then, will you get the results associated with the person you are now.

I started to act "as if now" when I decided that deep down inside I really was a writer.

Just to spook some of you a little bit, I recently had a beautiful past life regression session which confirmed that indeed writing has been a part of who I am for a very long time... So I started to really identify with that. I knew the outline of who I am supposed to be in this life was there, I was beginning to understand my purpose; now all I needed to do was pour myself into it.

I wrote every day of course (the good old-fashioned elbow grease action part); I wrote stories, NLP articles, blogs for my website, for LinkedIn, etc., and I also created an author Twitter account. I started to act as if I were already a successful writer, I started to think like one. Yes, as mentioned previously, sometimes it felt really kind of weird and crazy, and like I was losing the plot a little. But no matter. I kept believing in myself and what I could accomplish, and I kept at it.

I became a writer. This was not simply something I aspired to do anymore, it was simply who I was. Honestly, I would credit this as one of my biggest understandings.

Previously I had entertained this very misguided notion that "people like me" could not manifest their dreams. But after I started to get really good feedback on my articles, once I realised that I had made those results happen, I experienced a tremendous shift inside of me. There were no "people like them" and "people like me" anymore.

In NLP, through the process of modelling, we learn how to create excellence in our lives. We know that at any given moment in time, people are always much more than what they think they are, and also that we are all equal. We can all be excellent, we can all be successful, and we all have what it takes, deep inside, to achieve our dreams. And so all of a sudden I was in touch with my resources, living on purpose and getting the results that I wanted; and this is when I really understood the power of doing it "as if now."

By turning myself into the person I wanted to be, completely, without a single shred of doubt or resistance, I had attracted the results that went with it.

Absolutely awesome.

Another thing that successful people do is choose only empowering definitions. This also is not new! But now I have a better understanding of what it means. Because people "think positive", they work on their goals, they focus on what they want, but sometimes they neglect to look at the rules they have regarding success.

For example, some people believe that to be a successful author you have to write only a particular genre, get an advance from an "official" publisher, and sell at least X amount of copies.

Personally I think these people are just making life difficult for themselves. They have disempowering rules that are holding them back.

Successful people on the other hand will choose to believe that you can write the stuff you enjoy reading and that you know about; that you can publish and promote your book yourself; and that success will be achieved once a bunch of readers have a good time reading your story, and perhaps even learn something from it.

Now these are the people who get results.

So when you ask yourself, "What does success look like?" make sure that you define it in achievable terms too. Basically, make it smart! Create the perfect conditions for success, and then just go ahead and smash it!

★

TOP TIP # 6: CREATE A VISION BOARD

Ah, another one of my favourite things to do, and a lot of fun as well, especially on rainy Sunday afternoons when you have some time to yourself. If you live in England, pretty much you could do it every weekend!

If you find it a little hard to do visualisation exercises etc., I recommend you give vision boards a go.

All you do for this is get yourself a board, one of those cork ones would be good, or simply stick some A4 sheets together. Your board can be as small or as big as you like. What I often do with the ones I create is I take a picture of it when it is done and use it as a screen-saver on my laptop or my phone.

So, get yourself some magazines, and simply cut out the pictures that make you feel good; cut out the things that are related to your goals. For instance, if you are letting go of the fear of public speaking, create a board full of pictures of inspiring speakers, smiling, and looking happy and confident as they do their thing. Stick a photo of yourself in the middle of it.

If you are saving money for a new car, use pictures of your dream car; or your dream house if it is a new home you are working on. If your goal is to find the love of your life then find pictures of people in love, whatever love "looks like" for you.

Basically, you need to collect anything related to what you are working on creating in your life that makes you feel good and inspires you when you look at it. Give it some energy!

By the way, it does not have to be pictures only. You can stick words on your vision board if you like too. Again, so long as it is empowering stuff and makes you feel good, go ahead and use it.

You can have one vision board that reflects your life as a whole, or several boards for specific goals. That is up to you. Be creative with it and have fun!

Whether you then decide to share your board with the world or keep it private, do one very important thing: put it somewhere you can see it all the time. Look at it before you go to sleep at night. Put yourself into it, really feel the feelings of being that person, doing those activities, having those things. It will help to keep you focused on your goals, and stimulate your unconscious mind and Reticular Activating System.

★

TOP TIP # 7: GIVE AND BE GRATEFUL

Give to others. Give of yourself, your time, and your money. Share your knowledge. Share your experiences. And share your learnings so that you can learn from others too.

I was at the optician's a couple of years ago waiting for a check-up, and he had a sponsorship form on his table. He would be riding 100k on his bike for cancer research later on in the summer, and I hesitated. It had been one of these days at work when it seems like everybody was asking for money for one charity or another, and I thought, right, another one? I hesitated some more.

And then I told myself to stop being so ridiculous and to put my name down on the form. I was glad that I did.

Two minutes later my optician came in, said hello, and told me that they had forgotten to cancel my old contact lenses order, and so had received another six-months worth of them. Obviously he could have used them for himself, as samples or replacements etc.

Instead he just chose to give them to me, free of charge.

Wow!

I was really happy I had decided to sponsor him... imagine how bad I would have felt if I had decided not to and then been the recipient of his own generosity! I believe I got free contact lenses because I did exactly that: give.

Do good, be happy, and you will get good stuff in return. Remember how your reticular activating system works: you always get more of what you focus on. If you believe the world is a horrible place, if you believe everyone is out to get you, well, guess what...

Start to think and behave a little differently, and watch what happens. I have many more examples of happy, strange little incidents happening to me, including finding extra change in the coffee machine at work when I did not have enough money to buy myself one, or having a book delivered extra early when I really was not expecting it and really could not wait to get my hands on it...

That's when the Law of Attraction really does work, folks!

Also, be grateful for what you have, be grateful for this life. And celebrate your successes, big or small. Again, this is something you will have to get used to doing, and make time in your busy schedule to do. We are told to be "modest" and "keep quiet" about our achievements, but what is the point of that?? When you do good, when you achieve results, acknowledge that and give yourself a pat on the back.

You could start to write a journal for example, which

would also be a good way to keep track of the overall structure of your life, instead of getting lost in all the little details. Of course not everybody likes to write, so a journal could be a video blog or a Twitter account. Whatever works for you.

It is not just the huge events that matter, although they do of course. But the little things are wonderful too. Feeling the sun on your face, someone smiling at you, tasting a really great meal, being able to laugh, having a good friend, simply being alive…

What, you think your life is hard? You think it is rubbish? Well, make it good then! What are you waiting for? Start building the life of your dreams, right now! Like I said before, you can make it as hard or as wonderful as you want…

★

TOP TIP # 8: TAKE CARE OF YOURSELF

I get up at 05:30, five mornings a week, to get in a training run before work. And I enjoy it. What do you do?

If you want to be healthy, then exercising your body is absolutely essential. Because if your body is working well this means it will require less energy to function, energy that you can put into achieving your goals. That is the real reason you should want to be fit in the first place. When you are, your mind will run better. Obviously you do not have to do it everyday, but at least three times a week would be great. You can walk, run, go to the gym, dance, swim, do yoga, whatever you like. Thirty minutes per session will do. Just do something.

Getting your nutrition right is also essential in order to have a healthy body and a healthy mind. It is not about how you look, it is about how healthy you are. Eat organic as much as you can, eat balanced meals, eat lots of green and brown foods and stay away from ready-made and processed stuff.

These are the main rules. It does not have to be difficult! If you like, you can also go see a nutritionist, put a balanced and bespoke nutrition plan together. Again, like with exercise, make the time to really care for yourself.

Meditate!

Now, I only started to do it last year, and at first I thought I was doing it all wrong because I could not "dissolve in the bliss", that sort of thing, you know? But now I have understood it is not about that.

It is just about giving your mind a break, getting in touch with your inner core, learning to reconnect with your unconscious mind and your Higher Self, and making your brain stronger.

You can find meditation recordings online for free.

Like with exercise, you can do it everyday or just a few times a week, for five, ten, fifteen minutes, more if you have time. Take care of your body, take care of your mind, and be gentle with yourself.

Also, whilst we are on the subject, stop blasting away at yourself with thoughts of "not enough", or "I am so stupid"...

You are enough, you are good enough, you deserve to be loved, to be happy, to have a great job, and to enjoy your life. So every time one of those defeatist little thoughts pops into your head, just notice it, and let it go. It is fine to have those thoughts, so long as you do not latch on to to them and start ruminating on them and giving them power.

What I do is this, which I learnt to do with meditation:

Every time I start to doubt, to worry, to fear, what I do is I visualise the word in my head, then visualise myself blowing on it, and I watch it dissolve and float away.

Then I replace that word with a positive one, or even a sentence. Maybe something like, "I trust myself and my life, I am always safe, and excited about the opportunities coming my way."

Take a few slow, deep breaths, and meditate on this for a minute or so. Everytime I do, my state changes absolutely instantly, and I feel huge relaxation and well-being inside of me. This is how you shift your energy.

Why not write your own sentence and give it a try?

★

TOP TIP # 9: CREATE A GREAT ENVIRONMENT

Now, some people think that their genes affect everything in their lives, from their health, relationships, to what they can and cannot achieve. I think this is just another limiting decision myself. And I am not the only one.

Bruce Lipton, the author of *The Biology Of Belief,* is an American developmental biologist who is best known for his theory that genes and DNA can be influenced by a person's beliefs, and also by their environment.

Beliefs we have covered already, so let's take a look at your environment.

What I would ask you is, does it look and feel like your vision board? If not, time to redecorate! Feng Shui your entire house!

And obviously it does not have to be expensive: in my case all it took was a massive clear-up of some old junk I no longer needed in my flat, a good clean, a few colourful rugs, some nice pictures on the walls (my vision board is up there too), and lots and lots of green plants everywhere.

Make sure your environment stimulates your creativity as

well. Make sure that when you get home the place makes you feel good. Turn it into another world where all your dreams can be created, easily and effortlessly. Put some flow into your universe.

Your environment also means your friends and the people around you. Surround yourself with positive people who will support, empower, and inspire you. The moaners in the office will have to do without you, okay? Remember that after a while we start to become just like the people we hang out with: so choose wisely.

And last but not least, a final little tip about your environment: do you have a comfort zone?

Yes? Great! Now is the time to step out of it!

Jack Canfield famously says that "Most everything that you want is just outside your comfort zone," and "Everything you want is on the other side of fear." Bet you already knew this, right?

So start challenging yourself, do what scares you. Do one little thing every day, why not? Go say hi to someone you do not know and see what happens. Volunteer to do a presentation at work, why not!

I have already shared with you that I used to be terrified of public speaking, and so that is the only reason that I would not do NLP Trainers' Training. And yet I really wanted to share my story, I really wanted to train others in NLP, I really wanted to help people choose to think differently…

So I changed my belief and I did it anyway.

I love standing up in front of people these days! It is so much fun, so empowering, so wonderful to be able to share and connect with others through my work. Fear is not real. Learn to experience it and still do the things that you dream of doing.

Also, I suggest instead of watching the news, and TV shows like "Pointless" (I mean, hello???), instead turn to the Internet and start watching empowering stuff, programmes and interviews that will raise your consciousness and introduce you to new concepts, and ideas that will allow you to grow and evolve. I would suggest *www.liloumace.com* as a good source of eclectic and transforming material, and for the more daring amongst you, try *www.coasttocoastam.com*.

When it comes to the news… obviously you want to know what is going on in the world, but sometimes too much is just too much. For example, I was following the BBC Breaking News on Twitter, and I decided to stop. You do not need disaster after disaster landing on your phone every five seconds.

I would recommend using alternative sources of information as well, alternative TV networks, blogs and radio stations. Let's face it, if you really want to know what is going on out there you have to stop trusting the traditional media and go find out for yourself.

The truth is not at the BBC. They only tell you what they want you to know. So again, be savvy and use your critical mind to keep yourself informed. And obviously, read books!! Read empowering books. Read books about lots of different subjects. Keep your mind active and interested, there is always something new to learn.

For a list of books I have found incredibly helpful in my journey so far, please refer to the recommended reading section at the end of this book.

★

TOP TIP # 10: PUT IN 110% EFFORT

If you get your thinking right, and if you work hard, you will get the results that you want. It is as simple as that.

Trust yourself. Trust that you can do it. Whatever you can imagine you can achieve, remember? Do not let anybody tell you otherwise. Hire a coach and take action.

Put in the hours, do whatever you have to do, and keep the momentum going. I keep quoting Jack Canfield, and that is because he is once again spot-on when he says that "Satisfaction comes from enough action."

Here are a few examples of people who worked incredibly hard to achieve their dreams. This is borrowed from a blog written by Max Nisen at www.businessinsider.com:

- NBA legend Michael Jordan spent his off seasons taking hundreds of jump shots a day

- Starbucks CEO Howard Schultz continues to work from home even after putting in 13 hour days

- Dallas Mavericks owner Mark Cuban didn't take a

vacation for seven years while starting his first business

- American Idol host Ryan Seacrest hosts a radio show from 5 to 10 A.M. and runs a production company while appearing seven days a week on E!

- Venus and Serena Williams were up hitting tennis balls at 6 A.M. from the time they were 7 and 8 years old

And I love this very humbling story about James Robertson, from Detroit, Michigan. Talk about true grit.

Ten years ago when his old car broke down for good, he could not afford to get a new one. Robertson only makes $10.55 an hour, you see, and that was nowhere near enough. So what did he do? Get bitter, complain about it, join the moaners' club?

No.

Instead he decided that he was going to walk to work everyday: his work is twenty-one miles away from his home. Robertson, who is fifty-six years old, has been doing this for years now, everyday, no matter the weather, and it can get pretty nasty in Michigan!

He told *People Magazine*, "I don't think what I do is a big deal. I do what I have to do to get to work in the morning. It is just a part of my life."

He says it is all about determination and faith.

"My parents taught me a hard work ethic growing up in Detroit," he says. "It's all about keeping your schedule on track and focusing your mind on what matters."

★

CONCLUSION

Well, this is it, the end of my book. I am excited at the thought that my story is finally down on paper!

I thought long and hard before publishing this book about whether I really wanted to share my past and some of my present with… well, the people who know me, who I care about and whose opinion really matters to me; my future clients, and anybody out there who will buy the book. It was a big thing for me. I am a very private person, and I like to keep my stuff to myself, so this feels a little bit like walking into the office on a Monday morning completely naked!

But you know what, sometimes there is power in vulnerability, and I do believe that you have to be true to who you are. Live from the heart. Be yourself, and own every bit of it.

Also, the way that I discovered NLP, and the massively positive impact it has had on my life is too wonderful not to share. Last but not least, there is absolutely nothing wrong or shameful about mental health. We need to understand that we can all have healthy minds and lead happy lives; we can all learn how to do it, and we can all do it without the usual assortment of pills.

I learned recently that my grandfather was bipolar. I never got to know him because he committed suicide a few years before I was born. He did it by slitting his own throat. My cousin also suffers from the disorder. And I believe the seed was awakened inside of me too when I started on that downward spiral back in 2010... But, thanks to NLP, in my case the seed will never grow into a tree.

I have chosen to become a coach and trainer of NLP, precisely because I want to help other people through their challenges; and I know that I can do this because of what I went through myself, and what I learnt as a result.

Basically, I learned something that it seems very few people actually understand: that you can change your life, simply by choosing to think a little differently.

The vision I had for this book when I started to write it was simple. I wanted to make it very honest, and I wanted to make it very affordable. The aim was never to write an NLP manual or to invent and promote a radical new approach to happiness and well-being.

I just wanted to share a very personal story in the hopes that it will inspire people to see what you can achieve if you choose to think differently.

I will leave you with an article that I wrote a little while ago, which I found again the other day and decided would be a fitting end for this book.

I hope you like it, and thank you for reading.

With Love,
Nat

SECRET GIFT

I am laughing right now, and that is a good way to start the new year if you ask me.

I am laughing at myself because I spent a lot of idle time last year browsing articles on LinkedIn that talked about 'The Top 10 Reasons I Should Quit My Job In 2013'.

And today I am once again flicking through LinkedIn blogs, only this time the year has changed and I am reading about 'The Top 10 Reasons I Should Quit My Job In 2014'.

Thing is, I am still here and I have not quit. Damn. What is wrong with this picture? Have I been unconsciously procrastinating? Am I missing something, doing something wrong, or even worse, not doing enough??

I talked to a colleague recently about what I have been doing in 2013, mainly reading books, taking NLP trainings, writing, figuring things out, pondering, questioning, exploring, reading more books and writing some more.

Oh, the bliss… On the whole, feeling great and enjoying myself.

My colleague said she was glad (yeah, right!) that I seemed to think 2013 had been such a meaningful and productive year for me, but she was very quick to point out that I was still in the same job, living in the same flat, in the same old town, just the same as I was two years ago; so what had I accomplished, really? Where were the tangible results? And the money? And why the hell did I sound so happy about everything?

Well, some things can change very quickly, and I have had some of that in 2013 for sure.

Other things are on my list of longer-term goals and are expected to take a little bit more work, determination and tenacity. Some kind of good old-fashioned grit. And what is wrong with that? Absolutely nothing whatsoever.

Also, there is something else, which I have decided not to share with my colleague. Because I found something in 2013 that was not on my colour-coded Excel sheet of carefully written goals and precise timelines.

Something unexpected happened, and there was no Excel formula for it. I just made a discovery. I was given a gift.

It will not be obvious to the many impatient and quick-to-judge people in your life that you are working hard, when you are quietly and steadily building knowledge and resources in the background, acquiring invisible tools that will one day allow you to complete the big change you are dreaming of on the outside. Or just gently sorting things out for yourself.

J. R. R. Tolkien was spot-on target when he wrote that "Not all those who wander are lost".

If it takes you a little while to figure out (or remember) what it is that you really want in life, and who you really are at the core, so what?

It's your life!

In today's crazy-paced world it can seem extremely counter-productive to go 'on pause' for a bit. There is no time for that, correct? You got to keep moving, right?

Wrong.

Of course there is time. And I have been taking full advantage of it.

Because for some of us, all the gunk and false or not-quite-right ambitions we have accumulated over the years will need to be dealt with properly, before we can reconnect with our true passion. We have to separate the water from the mud first. Then we might find gold, figure out that thing that people call our Purpose. And everyone has one.

It is unique, and it is your own, and certainly not something you want to do simply because you are afraid of what might happen if you do not. Just the opposite in fact.

So when you find it, smile and keep quiet. Now is the time to stop, look and listen, adjust a little, then carry on with renewed energy and focus.

Whatever you do, pay no attention to anyone who suggests you are some kind of a joker because you are 'still here'. I am living proof that sometimes being 'still here' is the biggest achievement of all, and sometimes the only person who can truly assess how well you are doing is yourself.

Once you discover your life's purpose you will enjoy the ride no matter what, and as far as I am concerned this matters at least as much, if not more, as the final result.

So be happy, and truly savour the process of transforming yourself, away from the noise and the limelight.

If you want to reconnect with your true passion, forget LinkedIn, forget telling people about your goals, forget about proving things to a bunch of insignificant others.

Just look out for that precious gift, and when you find it grab on to it and start living with intent.

And have fun…

SWITCH ON!

QUOTES

"Common knowledge tells us that there is only one set order in the universe and only one set future for yourself. Then you're a victim and there is nothing you can do right? But this is what most people believe. Remember just one thing – common knowledge is just that: common, average, ordinary, unexceptional and usually second-rate."
Adriana James (www.nlpcoaching.com)

"But always, to her, red and green cabbages were to be jade and burgundy, chrysoprase and prophyry. Life has no weapons against a woman like that."
Edna Ferber

"So if you have a passion and aspire to greatness (…) wake up before dawn and apply yourself in silent anonymity. Practice your craft — in whatever shape or form that may be — late into the evening with relentless rigor (…) I can't promise that you will succeed in the way our culture inappropriately defines the term. But I can absolutely guarantee that you will become deeply acquainted with who you truly are. You will touch and exude passion. And discover what it means to be truly alive."
Rich Roll (www.richroll.com)

"Our environment, the world in which we live and work, is a mirror of our attitudes and expectations."
Earl Nightingale

QUOTES

"The two most important days in life are the day you are born and the day you discover the reason why."
Mark Twain

"Musicians must make music, artists must paint, poets must write if they are to ultimately be at peace with themselves. What human beings can be, they must be."
Abraham Maslow

"Remember always that you not only have the right to be an individual, you have an obligation to be one."
Eleanor Roosevelt

"Success is not the key to happiness. Happiness is the key to success. If you love what you are doing, you will be successful."
Albert Schweitzer

"The opposite of courage in our society is not cowardice, it is conformity."
Rollo May

RESOURCES - BOOKS

Here are some great books I would recommend:

- "Beyond Past Lives" – Mira Kelley
- "The Success Principles" – Jack Canfield
- "The Holographic Universe" – Michael Talbot
- "Think or Sink" – Gina Mollicone-Long
- "You Can Heal Your Life" – Louise Hay
- "The Biology of Belief" – Bruce Lipton
- "Quantum Healing" – Deepak Chopra
- "The Laughing Jesus" – Tim Freke
- "Women Who Run With Wolves" – Clarissa Pinkola Estes

RESOURCES - WEBSITES

- **www.switchonnlp.com:** Home of my Personal Development company. At "Switch On NLP" we believe that there are no unresourceful people, only unresourceful states. Get in touch and see what you can make happen!

- **www.inspire360.co.uk:** Home of the UK's leading school of NLP Training and Coaching Certification.

- **www.timfreke.com:** A unique voice in contemporary spiritual teaching. International best-selling author and stand-up philosopher.

- **www.nlpcoaching.com:** the Home of International, World Class trainings of NLP, Time Line Therapy®, Hypnosis, NLP Coaching and Adriana James' blogs.

- **www.liloumace.com:** Free web TV dedicated to awakening possibility, passion and purpose in people all around the world.

- **www.coasttocoastam.com:** UFOs, strange occurrences, life after death and other unexplained phenomena!

DEFINITIONS

ABNLP: the American Board of NLP

Belief: concepts that we decide are true. Convictions or agreements that certain things are true. Generalisations about the world.

Bipolar Disorder: Bipolar disorder, also known by its older name "manic depression," is a mental disorder that is characterized by serious mood swings. A person with bipolar disorder experiences alternating "highs" (what clinicians call "mania") and "lows" (also known as depression).

NLP: a model of communication. How we communicate to self and others - and how that communication creates and affects our behaviour.

Secondary Gain: when some apparently negative or problematic behaviour actually carries out some positive function at some other (often unconscious) level.

Time Line Therapy™: a powerful technique that we use in NLP to achieve great personal change and growth, by facilitating the elimination of the painful emotions attached to memories or events in the past. For example: anger, sadness, fear, hurt and guilt.

Time Line: the imaginary line that links your past, present and future, on which all your memories, past, present and future, are stored.

NOTES

NOTES

NOTES

NOTES

NOTES

ABOUT THE AUTHOR

Natalie Debrabandere is a writer, motivational speaker, coach and trainer of NLP, with a mission to facilitate positive change in her clients. She is the founder of Switch On NLP Limited, a coaching and personal development company based in Loughborough, UK, and she contributes regular articles and blogs to specialist NLP websites. When she is not writing or doing NLP, she enjoys dodging rain drops on her morning runs and spending long lazy hours creating the perfect home-made lasagne.

Contact: www.switchonnlp.com

18694157R00103

Printed in Great Britain
by Amazon